mr.
sunday's
soups

mr. sunday's soups

LORRAINE WALLACE

with BRIGIT BINNS

Photography by Alexandra Grablewski

WILEY

John Wiley & Sons, Inc.

Published by John Wiley & Sons, Inc.,
Hoboken, New Jersey

Published simultaneously in Canada

For general information about our other products and services, please contact our Customer Care Department within the United States at (877) 762-2974, outside the United States at (317) 572-3993 or fax (317) 572-4002.

Wiley also publishes its books in a variety of electronic formats. Some content that appears in print may not be available in electronic books. For more information about Wiley products, visit our web site at www.wiley.com.

Library of Congress Cataloging-in-Publication Data:

Wallace, Lorraine.
  Mr. Sunday's soups / Lorraine Wallace with Brigit Binns ; photography by Alexandra Grablewski.
    p. cm.
  Includes index.
  ISBN 978-0-470-64022-7 (pbk.); ISBN 978-0-470-94565-0 (ebk.); ISBN 978-0-470-94566-7 (ebk.); ISBN 978-0-470-94567-4 (ebk.)
  1. Soups. 2. Wallace, Chris. I. Binns, Brigit Legere. II. Title.
  TX757.W42 2011
  641.8'13—dc22

                          2010015686

Printed in the United States of America

10 9 8 7 6 5 4 3 2 1

To
Mr. Sunday
and our
beautiful family

Contents

Spring Favorites

Summer Favorites

Acknowledgments

I am grateful to the many dedicated and talented people who helped make this book possible.

Thank you:

My husband Chris and our children—Peter, Megan, Catherine, Andrew, Sarah, and Remick—for the love and encouragement that they give me unconditionally.

Mom, for teaching me to always use organic vegetables, and how to cook.

My family, for both recipes and memories: Mike and Mary Wallace, Kappy Leonard, Pauline and Richard Bourgeois, and Jennifer Wallace.

My friends the Dubins, Mariella Trager, Pamela Ginsberg, Arline Eltzroth, Tracy Hackett, Adam Maer, Ronald Braso, and Chantima Suka for sharing their favorite soups.

Chef Martin at Round Hill; the Hillwood Museum; the Jockey Club; Betsy Larsen of Larsen's Fish Market, and Frank Pellegrino of Rao's, for giving me recipes for soups that I have enjoyed at their establishments over the years.

My agent Michael Psaltis, of the Culinary Cooperative, who always helped me with the details and never let me lose sight of the big picture.

Brigit Binns, for her culinary artistry and her friendship.

My editor, Justin Schwartz, for his vision and professionalism.

My publisher, John Wiley & Sons, for believing in this project and making my vision come true with all their hard work.

Photographer Michael Bennett Kress, of MBK & Associates, for his keen eye.

Foreword

by Chris Wallace

Meals have always been important for the Wallace family.
When Lorraine and I married in 1997, we had to blend our two families. I had four children—she had two. And four of them were between the ages of 9 and 12. Our meals could be raucous affairs, but we were always together. And I don't think it's an overstatement to say we created our version of the Brady Bunch around the kitchen table.

In a sense, this was continuing a Wallace family tradition. When I was little, I didn't see much of my father, because my parents divorced early in my life. As I got older, so much of our getting to know each other involved meals. When I was thirteen, my father would take me every few weeks to Toots Shor's, a legendary watering hole in New York City where famous athletes hung out. To be honest, I was more excited about getting to see Frank Gifford or Willie Mays or Howard Cosell. But eventually, over slabs of roast beef, I got to know My Old Man. And gradually, this "stranger" became a big part of my life.

Now, we've had a very close relationship for decades. But still when I see him in New York or up in Martha's Vineyard in the summer, the best times—the times when we *really* talk—are at the table. For all the Wallaces, meals aren't just when we eat. It's where we congregate, catch up, and have our best conversations. It's where we live the traditions of our family.

Which brings me to *Mr. Sunday's Soups*. As Lorraine will tell you, Sunday Soup was her solution to the problem of how to get her busy teenager and her tired husband together on Sundays. It would be late in the morning when I'd come home from the studio, tired after getting up at 5:15 a.m. and grilling some big official. Remick would just be rolling out of bed and gearing up for an energetic day of sports. Soup was Lorraine's way to bring us together. And we all loved it.

Our Sunday Soups have become one of the most treasured times of my week. Here's how it goes: when I get home, I'm out of my suit and tie in about a minute, and then we all sit around the table to share our day—the one I've just had and the one Lorraine and Remick are beginning. We all enjoy one of Lorraine's wonderful soups (I never know what she is going to surprise me with that week). Then I go upstairs with the *Washington Post,* the *New York Times,* and Winston, our yellow Labrador. Soon, he's snoring by my side, while I'm reading the paper, and the sun is streaming into

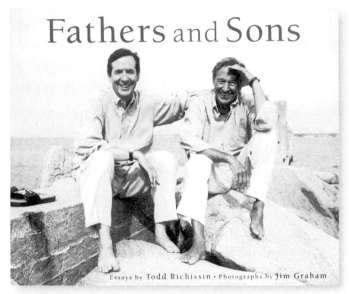

Father and Son: Chris and Mike. Photo by Jim Graham.

the bedroom. I'll read until I get tired, and then take a long nap. It's the soup, the paper, and the dog. And just writing about it, I get the warmest, happiest feeling. My job requires so much psychic energy and adrenaline. But now, I'm full of warm soup made by my favorite girl, reading the paper, my dog is sleeping beside me. It's the *best* part of the week.

Lorraine made soups before I started on the show, and they speak to my soul—they evoke a time and place, good times, and great friends. Chili makes me think of the Super Bowl. Lorraine will ask, "When's halftime?" and we'll all stream into the kitchen, then set up TV tables from the basement with bowls of chili and Lorraine's nachos. It's a wonderful family feeling. Whenever one of us gets sick, Lorraine is ready with a chicken soup—whether it's Chicken Noodle, Chinese Chicken Noodle, or Chicken Matzo Ball—I think of them as almost medicinal. Maryland Crab Soup always brings back the happy times we spend with some of our best friends in the summer—plus I love the taste.

I have a theory that, as a parent, the most important way you make an impression on your children is not what you say, but what you do. I came to know my father at the dinner table. And we built our family the same way. As you'll see, Lorraine's soups are much more than meals. They are an integral part of the Wallace family tradition. I hope they will bring you as much happiness and as many wonderful memories as they have for us.

Introduction

In 2003, my husband Chris accepted a position at Fox News to be the anchor of its political talk show, *Fox News Sunday*. Who knew our family would end up in the soup?

Let me explain. It was an incredible opportunity for Chris, and he was thrilled. But this decision turned around our family life, especially our weekend routine. Suddenly, Saturday nights were a time to get to bed early, not to go out. And after getting up at 5:15 Sunday mornings and questioning top national leaders, Chris would come home around 11:30 a.m., exhausted and hungry.

But for the rest of our family, weekends were still weekends. Our son Remick, then a freshman in high school, was hoping to be recruited by colleges to play baseball. Sunday mornings, he slept in (as teenagers do), then rushed out the door for workouts in the fall and winter, and games in the spring and summer.

Our young family: Remick, Sarah, Chris, Lorraine, Catherine, and Andrew. Photo by Leslie Cashen.

Peter, Megan, Andrew, Remick, and Sarah at Catherine's Graduation, University of St. Andrews, Scotland.

I was faced with a dilemma: how to feed both of my guys in a timely and nourishing manner, and how to bring our family together, even for a short time. The answer for us was soup—it was quick, easy, delicious, and good for you—and I served a different one each week. When my teenager rolled out of bed and my husband returned from doing his show, we would sit down for the short time we had to enjoy a family lunch. Even our yellow Labrador, Winston, would get into the act—happily slurping up a small bowl of warm soup.

This new tradition quickly grew a following. Our weekly meals together were a hit not just with our family, but also with many of our friends and colleagues. Chris bragged so much at work about going home to his hot soup that his coworkers at Fox started guessing what the soup of the week was. His colleagues even gave our ritual a name: "Soup Sunday," and Chris became Mr. Sunday, and I'm now Mrs. Sunday.

But it didn't stop there. Every Friday morning, Chris appears on *Fox and Friends* to promote his show for the upcoming weekend, and he often gets into a spirited and funny discussion with the show's hosts, Steve Doocy, Gretchen Carlson, and Brian Kilmeade. One Friday, Steve did the show from Washington. He asked the makeup ladies for some inside scoop to tease my husband, and they told him about our Soup Sunday tradition, adding that after his meal, Chris takes the papers—and the dog—up to bed for an afternoon nap. (After all, soup does make you sleepy!)

Now, in addition to our family, many friends ask me each week what Sunday Soup I am making. I hope my soups are delicious, but I know what people are responding to just as much is this wonderful way to bring family together. There doesn't seem to be a better time in America for Soup Sunday to become a new tradition: it's an affordable, healthy, and easy way for families to share a delicious meal. That's what I offer here in *Mr. Sunday's Soups.*

It's been seven years now since Chris started on *Fox News Sunday,* and this collection has been lovingly assembled and perfected over all that time. But I am always on the lookout for new, nourishing, fun, and delicious soups, because I love to cook. I truly enjoy finding the best local produce and ingredients to make recipes for my family. My husband marvels at how I can detect an herb or ingredient in a dish and identify it with such certainty. I often come home from a meal at a restaurant and remake the recipe, adding my own twist. Every soup you will read about in this book has its own story. Each one comes from a trip or a new food passion of mine. They come from our family's experiences—and sharing them has created new experiences.

Our Wedding Day: Megan, Peter, Chris, Lorraine, Remick, Catherine, Andrew, Sarah, and Bo. Photo by Marty Hublitz.

One of my favorite traditions is to combine a soup with a salad, but not the way you're used to seeing it served! My friends call it "Lorraine's Signature Soup-Salad." And for people who are trying to get vegetables into their diet, it's a great way to combine warmth and vitamins in one bowl. You take a creamy, semi-pureed soup and serve it hot, with a small, crisp salad tossed with fresh lemony vinaigrette served right on top of the soup. Trust me, it's a great combination of tastes and textures. When I was a child, my mother cooked English food, but I always wanted a salad! Suddenly I had the idea of putting salad on top of the soup (sometimes I put it underneath, too). It was a natural. Plus, it's a good way to sneak fresh vegetables into your children's diet without them noticing—or minding too much.

One of my simplest soups is Family Wellness Soup, which is great for treating colds and almost any other ailment. You take skinned, boneless chicken

Chris and Lorraine on our Wedding Day. Photo by Marty Hublitz.

thighs, add diced carrot, celery, and onion to the pot, and cover it with broth. After bringing it to a boil and then letting it simmer for one hour, you adjust the seasoning with salt and pepper. This is a natural cure-all and works wonders for speeding your loved ones along the road to recovery.

How do you feed your school-age children a nutrition-packed meal that's filling, local, and economical as well? Soup! In a lunch box thermos—why not? Make a big pot, then freeze it in small quantities, and defrost when you are ready—no fuss required. And I always know my kids are getting a warm and healthy meal.

I find it very exciting to create these wonderful soups for my family and friends. It is what I love to do. Over the years, I not only created soups, I collected them—mostly from friends, but also from great chefs whom I pestered after enjoying their specialties.

18

Winston's Nose

Winston, the yellow Labrador, is one of my biggest soup fans. I love to see his nose start to go up in the air when he knows the soup is almost ready. He stands by his special bowl, wagging his tail, and after I let the soup cool just a little bit, Winston always gets his share.

Chris and I are now empty-nesters—with all of our six children off to college or in the workplace. But whenever they come home, they always ask for their favorite soup. My soups helped to bring our expanded Wallace family together when the children were younger. And even today, they still love to come together around a big table, set with steaming bowls of soup. It's our very own tradition—and it's a tasty one!

The family on a crisp day out of golfing in St. Andrews, Scotland. Remick, Megan, Chris, Andrew, and Peter.

Fall Favorites

Hiking on a fall day out West. Sarah, Andrew, Catherine, and Remick.

Fall in Washington, D.C., is a very active time because suddenly everyone is back from vacation, and the government, businesses, and schools are in full swing. It's always an exciting time to reconnect with friends and family and hear about everyone's summer adventures. In October, Chris and I celebrate our wedding anniversary as well as birthdays for Remick, our grandson William, and Chris. It is a scheduling and social whirlwind for any mom to tackle—the back-to-school activities, sports, and extracurricular events can be overwhelming. Yet this is the season when I really start to get excited about the idea of creating new menus and dishes to feed my busy family.

Early fall usually kicks off with Indian summer, when the temperatures here in the D.C. area are cool in both the mornings and evenings, but the days are still warm. Farmer's markets and vegetable gardens are bursting with beautiful organic produce, just begging to be used in my favorite chowders, as well as my Fall Vegetable-Salad Soup, which combines potatoes, zucchini, and cauliflower with a crisp topping of arugula.

When the children were in middle school—and all the way through high school—I often drove from 2:30 in the afternoon until play rehearsals ended at 9:30 p.m. We had four children in three different schools, all quite a distance apart. Different friends and extracurricular activities for each child complicated the schedule further! Our evening meal was often delayed. That's when I started to prepare a soup for Friday night dinner. My Tortilla Soup is fun, colorful, and easy to prepare early in the day. Before I left the house in the afternoon, I'd set the table and preplate all the garnishes. When I walked in the door with tired and hungry kids, all that was left to do was cook the chicken. We were all able to enjoy a relaxing meal (even me!), with plenty of time to share the day's events. With six very verbal people around the table, I came up with a plan to avert chaos: everyone tells their favorite stories and memories in turn, going around the table one at a time (we always tell the least-favorite memories, too—after all, letting off steam is one of the great ways families cope with problems).

Fall is the season when we set our clocks back by one hour, and I find everyone gets a little harried and grumpy. Just when we have so much more to do in the day, the day gets shorter! This is when I pull out the true body warmers, like Turkey and Wild Rice Soup, Hearty Lentil Soup, and my recent favorite, "Pumpkin"-Pear Soup. All the soups in this chapter have helped to make our big family feel warm and safe, nourished, and loved.

Chris's mom: Kathy Leonard (a.k.a., Granny).

Chinese Chicken Noodle Soup

SERVES 6 TO 8 AS A MAIN DISH

Chris's mom, Kappy—or Granny, as we now all call her—loves to go out for Chinese meals. When we blended our two families into one, Fridays were often set aside for a "Friday Fun Night" with Granny. When the children had busy schedules and I was out carpooling from one sporting or theatrical event to another, I decided to create our own Chinese tradition by making this soup at home. To save time, I would make the broth and Cilantro-Mint Pesto ahead; then all that was left to do was to boil the noodles and serve. Add spring rolls and any other Chinese treat—fortune cookies are always a bonus—and you will have your own Friday Fun Night.

(recipe continues on page 24)

FOR THE BROTH

1 whole chicken (about 3½ pounds)

3 quarts (12 cups) low-sodium chicken broth, homemade (page 230) or store-bought

2 large pieces of zest from a scrubbed and dried lime

1 tablespoon crushed coriander seed

4 stalks lemongrass, thinly sliced

1 bay leaf

4 sprigs fresh mint

4 whole black peppercorns

¼ teaspoon chili powder

Kosher salt and freshly ground black pepper

TO SERVE

1 leek, white part only, well washed and thinly sliced

1 medium carrot, peeled and finely diced

One 10-ounce package Chinese noodles (mein)

Cilantro-Mint Pesto (recipe below)

CILANTRO-MINT PESTO

½ cup fresh cilantro (leaves and tender stems only)

½ cup fresh mint leaves

1 tablespoon extra-virgin olive oil

½ teaspoon kosher salt

1 teaspoon freshly ground black pepper

Rinse the chicken inside and out under cool running water; pat dry with paper towels.

In a 10-quart stockpot, combine the chicken, broth, lime zest, coriander seed, lemongrass, bay leaf, mint, peppercorns, chili powder, and ½ teaspoon salt. Place over medium-high heat and bring to a boil, then lower the heat and simmer, uncovered, for 1 hour. (Make sure the chicken is always submerged in the broth; add a little more water to keep it covered if necessary.)

Lift the cooked chicken from the broth and set aside to cool. When cool enough to handle, remove and discard all the skin and bones. Shred the meat with two forks and set aside.

Strain the broth through a colander lined with cheesecloth, and place in a clean soup pot. Season with salt and pepper to taste.

To serve, return the broth to a simmer and add the shredded chicken, leek, and carrot. Cook until vegetables are tender, about 5 minutes.

Meanwhile, bring a saucepan of salted water to a boil and cook the noodles for 3 minutes; drain well and rinse under cool water to keep them from sticking.

Divide the noodles among warm bowls and ladle the soup over the noodles. Garnish with a dollop of Cilantro-Mint Pesto.

To Make Pesto: In a small food processor, combine all the ingredients. Pulse until smooth. If not serving immediately, cover and refrigerate for up to 24 hours.

Chicken Matzo Ball Soup

SERVES 6

Here is a soup to feed the fall soul. The clear chicken broth, soft vegetables, and fluffy matzo balls make this soup perfect for any fall lunch or dinner. Our family enjoys this soup so much that I adopted a simpler approach: by using the Manischewitz Matzo Ball Mix right from the box, I can serve it more frequently when the weather begins to change during the fall season. I like to prepare both the broth and matzo balls early in the day (just make the matzo mix and refrigerate until you get home). When you're ready, make the balls and drop them into boiling water. This is the perfect satisfying meal for hungry children when they come home from school.

- 1 whole chicken (about 3½ pounds)
- 2 medium onions, roughly chopped
- 4 carrots, peeled and thickly sliced
- 2 stalks celery, thickly sliced
- 2 parsnips, peeled and thickly sliced
- 1 bay leaf
- 1 bunch fresh dill, coarsely chopped, plus extra for garnish
- 3 tablespoons finely chopped fresh parsley, plus extra for garnish
- Kosher salt and freshly ground black pepper
- One 4.5-ounce box Manischewitz Matzo Ball & Soup Mix
- 2 large eggs
- 2 tablespoons canola oil

Rinse the chicken under cool water inside and out; dry with paper towels. Place in a large, heavy soup pot or Dutch oven and add the onions, carrots, celery, parsnips, bay leaf, dill, and parsley.

Cover the ingredients with about 1 inch of water and bring to a boil; reduce the heat to medium-low and simmer, partially covered, for about 2 hours. (Skim the surface every so often with a large, flat spoon to remove foam.) Season to taste with salt and pepper and set aside to cool.

When cool enough to handle, remove the chicken and set aside. Skim the fat from the top of the stock and strain the broth, reserving the vegetables. Discard the bay leaf. Return the stock and vegetables to the pot.

Shred the cooled chicken, discarding bones and fat, and return the chicken and any accumulated juices to the pot.

Meanwhile, make the matzo balls according to the package directions, using the eggs and canola oil as directed.

When ready to serve, warm the soup and add the matzo balls. Ladle into warm bowls, garnish with a little dill and parsley, and serve immediately.

> **TIP**
> *If you plan to make this soup frequently, you can buy a larger box of matzo ball mix; follow the instructions on the label. What could be easier!*

Chicken Noodle Soup

SERVES 6

This is one of the first soups I learned to cook. I used to pack this in our children's lunch pails, so they would have a warm treat on a cool fall day. It's a beautifully simple way to make your family feel good, while they're eating healthy. I like to serve Chicken Noodle Soup with saltine crackers or toast.

2 quarts (8 cups) low-sodium chicken broth, homemade (page 230) or store-bought

2 small boneless skinless chicken breasts (about 7 ounces each)

1½ cups finely chopped onion

3 carrots, peeled, halved, and thinly sliced

3 stalks celery, thinly sliced

4 ounces dried thin egg noodles (about half an 8.8-ounce package)

4 tablespoons finely chopped fresh flat-leaf parsley, divided

Kosher salt and freshly ground black pepper

Place a large, heavy soup pot or Dutch oven over medium-high heat and add the broth. Bring to a simmer, then add the chicken breasts and immediately remove the pan from the heat. Cover and let stand until tender, about 12 minutes.

Lift the chicken breasts from the broth and let them cool on a plate. Cut into 1-inch pieces and set aside.

Return the broth to a simmer over medium heat and add the onion, carrots, and celery. Simmer until the vegetables are tender, about 10 minutes, skimming off any foam that rises to the surface.

Add the chicken pieces, noodles, and 2 tablespoons of the parsley to the broth; season with salt and pepper to taste.

As soon as the noodles are tender, ladle into warm bowls or tall mugs, sprinkle with the remaining 2 tablespoons parsley, and serve immediately with large spoons to capture all the noodles and tasty chicken.

Minestrone and Arugula Salad Soup

SERVES 6

This is one of my signature soup-salad recipes. It's a veggie-and-bean-packed minestrone, high in protein and low in fat. The mixture of the warm soup and the cold salad makes for a perfectly balanced Sunday lunch. Our family prefers arugula, but any mixed salad greens can be used instead.

Arugula is in abundance at our DuPont farmer's market at the beginning of fall. I love going to the market on Sundays after Chris's show to gather the best organic ingredients to feed our family for the week.

(recipe continues on page 30)

3 tablespoons extra-virgin olive oil, divided

3 ounces thinly sliced pancetta, finely chopped

2 medium shallots, finely chopped

2 stalks celery, finely chopped

1 medium onion, finely chopped

1 large carrot, peeled and finely chopped

½ fennel bulb, cored and finely chopped (see Tip below)

4 garlic cloves, minced

½ teaspoon red pepper flakes

2 bay leaves

2 tablespoons tomato paste

One 14-ounce can diced tomatoes, with juice

One 15-ounce can Great Northern beans, rinsed and drained

1 quarts (4 cups) low-sodium chicken broth, homemade (page 230) or store-bought

Kosher salt and freshly ground black pepper

1 cup loosely packed baby arugula leaves

½ cup fresh flat-leaf parsley leaves

1 tablespoon fresh lemon juice

Place a large, heavy soup pot or Dutch oven over medium heat and add 2 tablespoons of the oil. Add the pancetta and cook, stirring occasionally, until crisp, about 5 minutes. Stir in the shallots, celery, onion, carrot, and fennel; cook, stirring occasionally, until softened, 5 to 6 minutes.

Stir in the garlic, pepper flakes, and bay leaves and cook until fragrant, about another minute. Stir in the tomato paste and cook, stirring, for 2 minutes more.

Stir in the tomatoes with their juice, the beans, and broth. Bring to a boil, then reduce the heat to low and simmer gently, partially covered, for 1 hour.

Discard the bay leaves; season with salt and black pepper to taste.

To serve: In a bowl, toss the arugula and parsley with the lemon juice and remaining 1 tablespoon of oil. Season the salad with salt and black pepper to taste. Ladle the soup into wide, warm bowls and top with some of the salad.

TIP
If the feathery green fronds are still attached to the fennel, chop a tablespoonful and add to the arugula and parsley mixture when serving.

Butternut Squash Puree

SERVES 4

This is a simple version of butternut squash soup: instead of wrestling with a whole squash, I prefer to cut the squash in half and roast it in the oven to soften the flesh, then use this as the basis to create this simple soup. It is perfect for a lovely fall lunch, and I sometimes serve this bright yellow soup as the starter for a fall dinner party. Here's a fun and festive idea: serve popovers instead of bread alongside this soup (recipe follows).

3 pounds butternut squash (about 1½ large squash)

5 tart apples, such as Granny Smith, peeled, cored and cut into chunks

4 tablespoons extra-virgin olive oil, divided

¼ cup water

2 leeks, white parts only, well washed and finely chopped

1¼ quarts (5 cups) low-sodium chicken or vegetable broth, homemade (page 230 or 231) or store-bought

Kosher salt and freshly ground black pepper

2 tablespoons finely snipped fresh chives

TIP

Always allow soup to cool for 5 to 10 minutes before pureeing in a blender, and hold the top of the blender firmly with a folded towel before you switch on the machine. Otherwise, the hot soup may expand and you'll end up with a messy explosion!

Preheat the oven to 350°F.

Halve the squash lengthwise and scrape out the seeds and fibers. Carefully remove the peel and cut the flesh into 1-inch chunks.

In a roasting pan, combine the squash and apples. Drizzle with 2 tablespoons of the oil, and toss until evenly coated. Pour the water around the edge of the pan and roast, stirring occasionally, until the squash and apples are tender, about 1 hour.

Meanwhile, place a large skillet over medium heat and add the remaining 2 tablespoons oil. Add the leeks and cook, stirring occasionally, until tender and slightly golden, 10 to 12 minutes.

In a blender or food processor, combine the roasted squash and apples, the leeks, and 1 cup of the broth. (See Tip below.) Process, scraping down the sides of the bowl as necessary, until very smooth, about 20 seconds. (Hold the top of the blender firmly with a folded towel to prevent an explosion of hot soup.)

Transfer the puree to a large, clean soup pot. Stir in the remaining 4 cups broth and bring to a simmer over medium heat just to warm through. Season with salt and pepper to taste.

Ladle the soup into wide, warm bowls. Garnish with the chives and serve immediately.

(recipe continues on page 35)

BLUE CHEESE POPOVERS

Nonstick cooking spray

1 cup all-purpose flour

1 tablespoon finely chopped fresh flat-leaf parsley

½ teaspoon salt

¼ teaspoon ground white pepper

1¼ cups whole milk, at room temperature

2 large eggs, at room temperature

1 tablespoon butter, melted

3 ounces creamy blue cheese, crumbled

Preheat the oven to 450°F and place a rack in the bottom third of the oven. Spray a 24-cup, nonstick mini-muffin pan generously with the cooking spray.

In a medium bowl, whisk together the flour, parsley, salt, and pepper. In a separate medium bowl, whisk together the milk, eggs, and butter. Pour the milk mixture over the flour mixture and whisk together until just combined (don't worry if there are a few lumps). Pour the batter into the prepared muffin cups to within about ¼ inch of the top. Top each cup with a pinch of the blue cheese.

Bake for 10 minutes without opening the oven door. Reduce the heat to 350°F and bake until golden brown and nicely puffed, 8 to 10 minutes more.

> **TIP**
> *Do not attempt this recipe unless you have nonstick mini-muffin pans!*

Butternut Squash Chowder

SERVES 8

This recipe makes use of butternut squash puree, but here I finish the soup with a nice hearty helping of chowder ingredients: potatoes, cream, and bacon. Our family loves this soup on a crisp fall day when energetic children and adults all need a little more taste and warmth to satisfy their hunger.

2 medium butternut squash, halved lengthwise

4 slices bacon, cut into ½-inch strips

1 medium yellow onion, coarsely chopped

2 stalks celery, coarsely chopped

1 bay leaf

1 teaspoon finely chopped fresh sage, plus extra for garnish

2 russet potatoes, peeled and cut into ½-inch cubes

¼ cup dry white wine

1 quart (4 cups) low-sodium chicken broth, homemade (page 230) or store-bought

1 tablespoon kosher salt

1 teaspoon freshly ground black pepper

½ cup heavy cream

TIP

Make the soup one day in advance, up to but not including the step when you add the cream; cool, cover, and refrigerate. When ready to serve, reheat the soup and add the cream.

Preheat the oven to 350°F. Line a roasting pan with aluminum foil.

Lay the butternut squash halves face down on the foil. Prick the skin of the squash with a fork in several places. Bake for 45 minutes, or until tender. Set aside to cool.

Place a large, heavy soup pot or Dutch oven over medium heat and add the bacon. Cook, stirring frequently, until crisp, about 5 minutes. Using a slotted spoon, transfer the bacon to a paper towel–lined plate and set aside.

Pour off and discard all but 1 tablespoon of the fat from the pot and return to medium heat. Add the onion, celery, bay leaf, and sage and cook, stirring occasionally, just until the vegetables are tender but not browned, 5 to 6 minutes. Stir in the potatoes and cook for 3 minutes more.

Add the wine and simmer for 2 minutes, stirring to scrape up the browned bits. Add the broth, salt, and pepper. Bring to a boil, then reduce the heat to low and simmer gently, partially covered, until the potatoes are tender, about 10 minutes.

Remove any seeds or stringy membranes from the butternut squash halves and scoop the flesh into a large bowl. With a potato masher, mash until smooth. Stir the squash puree and reserved bacon into the soup pot, bring to a simmer, and let cook for 2 to 3 minutes, just to blend the flavors. Stir in the cream and taste for seasoning; adjust the salt and pepper as necessary. Discard the bay leaf.

Ladle the chowder into warm bowls and garnish with a pinch of the remaining sage.

Turkey and Wild Rice Soup

SERVES 10

We just love the combination of wild rice with turkey, and both appear frequently in our family meal planning. I created this simple recipe to incorporate these two favorite foods. This is a good soup to pack for school lunches, or enjoy at home on a crisp fall afternoon with a wedge of crusty eighteen-grain bread.

2 tablespoons extra-virgin olive oil

3 leeks, white and light green parts only, well washed and coarsely chopped

2 carrots, peeled and coarsely chopped

1 stalk celery, coarsely chopped

3 garlic cloves, minced

2 pounds boneless skinless turkey thighs (about 3 thighs)

2 quart (8 cups) low-sodium chicken broth, homemade (page 230) or store-bought

1¼ cups cooked wild rice (see Tip below)

2 tablespoons low-sodium soy sauce

3 tablespoons finely chopped fresh flat-leaf parsley

Kosher salt and freshly ground black pepper

Place a large, heavy soup pot or Dutch oven over medium heat and add the oil. Add the leeks and cook, stirring occasionally, until tender but not browned, 5 to 7 minutes. Stir in the carrots, celery, and garlic and cook, stirring, for 1 minute more.

Add the turkey thighs and broth and bring to a boil. Reduce the heat to low and simmer until the turkey thighs are firm and cooked through with no pink remaining in the center, about 1 hour. Lift the turkey from the pot and, when cool enough to handle, use two forks to shred the meat into bite-size pieces. Return the meat to the soup pot.

Stir in the wild rice, soy sauce, and parsley and simmer for 5 minutes more.

Season with salt and pepper to taste. Ladle the soup into warm bowls and serve.

TIP
Wild rice is easy to cook but takes quite a long time—usually about 45 minutes.

Turkey Soup with Barley and Mushrooms

SERVES 8

Here, I created a more elaborate version of my Turkey and Wild Rice Soup (preceding recipe). I like to cook with dried mushrooms, which add fantastic flavor to any dish. My mother is English, so barley has always been a favorite grain—I grew up eating it in soups and stews. She always said it was a good source of gluten, "great for your hair and nails."

You may also use quick-cooking barley, which cooks in 10 to 12 minutes; follow the instructions on the package. For extra flavor, substitute ½ cup of the mushroom-soaking liquid for ½ cup of the water, when cooking the barley.

1 ounce mixed dried mushrooms

2 tablespoons extra-virgin olive oil

3 leeks, white parts only, well washed and coarsely chopped

1 pound white button or cremini mushrooms, brushed clean and coarsely chopped

2 carrots, peeled and coarsely chopped

3 garlic cloves, minced

2 pounds boneless skinless turkey thighs (about 3 thighs)

2 quart (8 cups) low-sodium chicken broth, homemade (page 230) or store-bought

1½ cups water

¼ teaspoon kosher salt

½ cup pearl barley (see headnote opposite)

2 teaspoons Worcestershire sauce

3 tablespoons finely chopped fresh flat-leaf parsley

Freshly ground black pepper

TIP

Always use the flavorful "broth," i.e., the mushroom-soaking liquid, left over after you have reconstituted dried mushrooms.

Soak the dried mushrooms in 2 cups of boiling water for 30 minutes. Drain the soaked mushrooms, reserving the soaking liquid. Strain the liquid through a fine-mesh sieve or cheesecloth to remove any grit. Dice the mushrooms and set aside.

Place a large, heavy soup pot or Dutch oven over medium heat and add the oil. Add the leeks and cook, stirring occasionally, until tender but not browned, 5 to 7 minutes. Stir in the white button mushrooms, soaked mushrooms, carrots, and garlic and cook, stirring, for 2 minutes more.

Add the turkey thighs, broth, and 1 cup of the mushroom-soaking liquid and bring to a boil. Reduce the heat to low, cover, and simmer until the turkey is firm and cooked through, with no pink remaining in the center, about 1 hour.

Meanwhile, bring the water to a boil in a small saucepan and add the salt. Add the barley, reduce the heat to low, cover, and simmer gently until all the liquid is absorbed and the barley is tender, about 45 minutes. If there is still liquid in the pan, drain the barley well.

Lift the turkey from the pot and, when cool enough to handle, cut the meat into bite-size pieces. Return the meat to the pot and add the cooked barley.

Stir in the Worcestershire sauce and parsley and simmer 5 minutes more. Season with salt and pepper to taste.

Ladle the soup into warm bowls and serve.

Hearty Lentil Soup

SERVES 6 TO 8

This is perhaps Mr. Sunday's all-time favorite soup—and that's saying a lot, because he loves them all! Chris really likes lentils— in every color, and prepared in every way. He feels they warm his body and soul. I first created this soup because it is low in fat and high in protein, but we would enjoy it no matter what, especially on a cold fall or winter day! The curry powder here adds just the right amount of spice, and I often like to garnish my lentil soup with a slice of lemon at serving time, for a fresh and pretty note.

1 cup dried lentils

1¼ quarts (5 cups) low-sodium chicken broth, homemade (page 230) or store-bought

1 onion, finely chopped

1 stalk celery, finely chopped

1 carrot, peeled and finely chopped

1 garlic clove, minced

1 green bell pepper, cored, seeded, and finely chopped

1 small potato, peeled and roughly chopped

2 cups tomato sauce

½ teaspoon curry powder

½ teaspoon dried basil

1 teaspoon kosher salt

Freshly ground black pepper

Rinse the lentils well in a colander and pick over and discard any discolored lentils or debris.

In a large, heavy soup pot or Dutch oven, combine the lentils, broth, onion, celery, carrot, and garlic. Bring to a boil, then reduce the heat to low and simmer, covered, until the vegetables are just tender, about 30 minutes.

Add the bell pepper, potato, tomato sauce, curry powder, basil, salt, and black pepper to taste. Continue to simmer until the potato is cooked, about 15 minutes more.

Ladle into warm bowls or tall mugs and serve.

Senate Bean Soup

Adapted from the recipe on the U.S. Senate web site

SERVES 8

Bean soup is on the menu in the U.S. Senate's restaurant every day and has been a favorite among our nation's lawmakers since about 1903! Opinions differ on its origins—some say Senator Fred Dubois of Idaho was the first to repeatedly request this soup, while others credit Senator Knute Nelson of Minnesota for its popularity. No matter who was the first to champion this soup, it's safe to say it will never disappear from the menu. If you are lucky enough to be invited to this famous dining room, you must try this historic favorite. A cup of this navy bean soup is a Washington must!

(recipe continues on page 46)

2 pounds dried navy beans
4 quarts (16 cups) water
1½ pounds smoked ham hocks
2 tablespoons butter
1 onion, finely chopped
1 tablespoon kosher salt
Freshly ground black pepper

In a colander, rinse the beans under hot running water until they appear slightly whitened. Pick out and discard any bad ones or debris.

In a large, heavy soup pot or Dutch oven, combine the beans, water, and ham hocks and place over medium-high heat. Bring to a boil, then reduce the heat to low, cover, and simmer gently, stirring occasionally, until the beans are tender, about 3 hours.

Lift out the ham hocks and, when cool enough to handle, remove and dice the meat. Discard the fat, bone, and gristle and return the meat to the pot.

In a small skillet, warm the butter over medium heat. Add the onion and cook, stirring, until slightly golden, 3 to 5 minutes. Stir the onion into the soup, along with the salt and pepper to taste. Bring to a simmer and taste for seasoning. Ladle into warm bowls and serve.

Tortilla Soup

SERVES 8

I first discovered tortilla soup on a visit to the renowned Mansion on Turtle Creek in Texas many years ago. After returning home, I decided to re-create the soup, and it quickly became a part of the Wallace family tradition. This is the soup our daughter Sarah requests most! I love to serve this to our family because the broth is both light and warming, and the colorful garnishes provide all the necessary food groups to make an entire meal in a bowl. In a slight departure from tradition, we use corn chips instead of frying strips of corn tortillas (which can be messy!).

Sometimes, for an elegant and festive start to a dinner party, I make the broth as directed below, and simply garnish with sliced avocado. Yummy either way!

(recipe continues on page 49)

3 tablespoons corn oil

4 small corn tortillas, coarsely chopped

6 garlic cloves, minced

3 tablespoons roughly chopped fresh cilantro (leaves and tender stems only)

1 cup onion puree (see Tip below)

2 cups fresh tomato puree (see Tip below)

1 tablespoon ground cumin

2 teaspoons chili powder

2 bay leaves

2 quarts (8 cups) low-sodium chicken broth, homemade (page 230) or store-bought

2 teaspoons kosher salt

Cayenne pepper

GARNISHES

2 cooked chicken breasts, cut into 1-inch cubes (see Tip below)

2 avocados, peeled, pitted, and diced

1½ cups shredded Cheddar cheese

2 cups tortilla chips, such as Tostitos

Place a large, heavy soup pot or Dutch oven over medium heat and add the oil. Add the tortillas, garlic, and cilantro and cook until soft, about 5 minutes. Add the onion and tomato purees, and bring to a boil. Stir in the cumin, chili powder, bay leaves, and broth.

Return the soup to a boil, then reduce the heat to low and simmer, uncovered, until slightly thickened, about 30 minutes. Stir in the salt and cayenne to taste.

Remove the soup from the heat and let cool slightly. Strain the soup through a fine-mesh sieve or a colander lined with cheesecloth into a separate soup pot; discard the solids. Ladle the strained soup into warm bowls.

Garnish each bowl with the chicken, avocado, cheese, and tortilla chips, dividing the garnishes evenly. Serve immediately.

TIPS

• *Make the soup one day ahead, and gently heat the tortilla broth just before serving.*

• *Cook the chicken breasts according to the instructions on page 25.*

• *To make onion puree: Peel a medium onion and cut it into large chunks. In a food processor, pulse until completely smooth—almost watery—scraping down the sides of the bowl as necessary to make a completely smooth puree.*

• *To make tomato puree: Core 6 plum or Roma tomatoes and cut into large chunks. Puree as for the onions above; there is no need to wash the food processor bowl in between.*

Creamy Mushroom Soup

SERVES 6

Mushrooms are in great abundance at the Dupont farmer's market, which I visit most Sunday mornings after Chris's show. I just had to create an old fashioned–style creamy mushroom soup to use these delicate morsels. As far as I'm concerned, this soup cries out for a smoked turkey sandwich on multigrain bread! Bon appétit!

- 1 ounce dried porcini or morel mushrooms
- 1½ quarts (6 cups) low-sodium chicken broth, homemade (page 230) or store-bought
- 8 tablespoons (1 stick) butter
- 1 yellow onion, finely chopped
- 1½ pounds cremini mushrooms, brushed clean and sliced
- ⅓ cup all-purpose flour
- 1 tablespoon soy sauce
- 1½ cups half-and-half
- ¼ cup tawny port (optional)
- 2 teaspoons kosher salt
- Freshly ground black pepper
- 2 tablespoons finely chopped fresh flat-leaf parsley, for garnish

TIPS
- *You can make this soup up to 2 days in advance; reheat gently to serve.*
- *Adding the optional port gives this soup flavor and sophistication.*

In a medium saucepan, combine the dried mushrooms and 4 cups of the broth.

Cover and bring to a boil over medium heat, then reduce the heat to low and simmer for 5 minutes. Remove from the heat and set aside.

Place a large, heavy soup pot or Dutch oven over medium heat. Add the butter and, when it has melted, add the onion and cook, stirring, until tender, about 5 minutes. Add the cremini mushrooms and cook, stirring, until tender, 3 to 5 minutes more.

Sprinkle the flour over the onion-mushroom mixture, stirring until it is incorporated and the mushrooms are coated, about 1 minute more. Add the remaining 2 cups of broth in a thin stream, stirring all the time.

Strain the soaked mushrooms through a colander lined with damp cheesecloth to remove any grit. Add the strained broth, soaked mushrooms, and soy sauce to the soup pot and simmer until the mushrooms are tender and the flavors have blended nicely, about 15 minutes.

Remove the soup from the heat and let cool slightly. Transfer about 2½ cups of the soup mixture, with plenty of the vegetables, to a blender or food processor. Puree until smooth and creamy. (Hold the top of the blender firmly with a folded towel to prevent an explosion of hot soup.)

Return the pureed soup to the pot and stir in the half-and-half, port (if using), salt, and pepper to taste. Return the soup to a simmer and taste for seasoning. Adjust the salt and pepper as desired. Ladle the soup into warm bowls, garnish with a big pinch of the parsley, and serve immediately.

Fall Vegetable-Salad Soup

SERVES 8

Here is another wonderful example of one of my signature soup-salad recipes. Both zucchini and fingerling potatoes are abundant at the beginning of fall. Our family loves the earthy and delicious flavor of the vegetables and chickpeas. I chose arugula for this recipe because the peppery taste adds amazing zest!

2 tablespoons extra-virgin olive oil

3 leeks, white parts only, well washed and finely chopped

6 small zucchini, halved lengthwise and thinly sliced

8 ounces fingerling or new potatoes, scrubbed and thinly sliced

1 large cauliflower, trimmed and roughly chopped

1½ quarts (6 cups) low-sodium chicken broth, homemade (page 230) or store-bought

1 teaspoon kosher salt

Freshly ground black pepper

One 15-ounce can chickpeas, rinsed and drained

2 tablespoons fresh lemon juice

8 cups loosely packed baby arugula leaves

Finely grated zest from a scrubbed and dried lemon

2 tablespoons roughly chopped fresh flat-leaf parsley

Place a large, heavy soup pot or Dutch oven over medium heat and add the oil. Add the leeks and cook, stirring occasionally, until softened, about 5 minutes.

Add the zucchini, potatoes, and cauliflower. Cook, stirring occasionally, until slightly softened, about 8 minutes. Add the broth, salt, and pepper to taste.

Bring the soup to a boil, then reduce the heat to low and simmer gently, partially covered, until the vegetables are very tender, about 20 minutes. Stir in the chickpeas and cook for 3 minutes more. Stir in the lemon juice.

Place a cup of arugula in each wide, shallow bowls and ladle the soup over the top. Scatter the lemon zest and parsley over the top.

Carrot Soup with Sage and Popcorn

This is a wonderful soup to bring your family together in the kitchen—every age group can get involved! Just watch their faces as they pop the popcorn—not to mention that they will truly benefit from all the good beta-carotene you are serving them!

(recipe continues on page 55)

4 tablespoons (½ stick) butter, divided

2 tablespoons extra-virgin olive oil

1 large onion, coarsely chopped

1 quart (4 cups) low-sodium vegetable or chicken broth, homemade (page 230 or 231) or store-bought

1 quart (4 cups) water

2 pounds carrots, peeled and sliced ⅓ inch thick

2 teaspoons kosher salt

Freshly ground black pepper

½ cup heavy cream

½ cup whole milk

12 fresh sage leaves

1 cup popped popcorn

TIP
The carrot soup can be refrigerated overnight; reheat gently and adjust the seasoning prior to serving.

Place a large, heavy soup pot or Dutch oven over medium-low heat. Add 1 tablespoon of the butter and the oil; when the butter has melted, add the onion and cook, stirring occasionally, until softened, about 5 minutes.

Add the broth, water, and carrots and bring to a boil over high heat. Reduce the heat to low, cover, and simmer gently until the carrots are tender, about 30 minutes. Stir in the salt and pepper to taste.

Remove the soup from the stove and uncover the pan. Let cool for at least 5 minutes.

Working in batches, process the soup in a blender or food processor until smooth. (Hold the top of the blender firmly with a folded towel to prevent an explosion of hot soup.) As you puree each batch, transfer it to a clean soup pot.

Stir in the cream and milk and warm the soup through gently over medium heat. Taste for seasoning and adjust with salt and pepper as necessary.

In a small skillet, warm the remaining 3 tablespoons butter over medium heat. When the butter is foaming, add the sage leaves and stir until crisp, about 1 minute. Transfer the sage leaves to a paper towel with a slotted spoon, and continue to cook the butter until it is golden brown, about 2 minutes more (watch carefully, so it doesn't burn). Remove from the heat.

Ladle the soup into wide, warm bowls and garnish with the sage leaves, a drizzle of the browned butter, and the popcorn.

"Pumpkin"-Pear Soup

SERVES 8

I find sweet potatoes much easier to handle than pumpkin, and the flavor and color are almost exactly the same—if not better, in certain seasons—than pumpkin. But I also love the sound of "pumpkin" soup in the fall. Diners need never know you took the easy route! Here, I add Bartlett pears and prosciutto, for a sweet and salty complement to the earthy sweet potato flavor. The maple cream finishes this silky soup, making it a succulent first course for a late fall lunch or dinner.

TIPS
• Pumpkin can be stringy and tough in the fall. I love to make this soup with sweet potato, but, if desired, substitute kabocha squash or butternut squash for the sweet potato. The color will still be beautiful and pumpkin-like.
• To make this into a vegetarian soup, simply omit the prosciutto, choose vegetable broth, and finish with a few croutons and a tiny sprig of fresh thyme.

(recipe continues on page 58)

Nonstick cooking spray

2 pounds sweet potatoes, peeled and cut into 1½-inch chunks (see Tip on page 56)

2 tablespoons extra-virgin olive oil

3 ounces thinly sliced prosciutto, halved lengthwise and cut into thin strips

1 medium yellow onion, finely chopped

1 tablespoon light brown sugar

½ teaspoon ground cumin

2 quarts (8 cups) low-sodium chicken or vegetable broth, homemade (page 230 or 231) or store-bought

½ teaspoon kosher salt

2 ripe Bartlett pears, peeled, cored, and coarsely chopped (about 2 cups)

¼ cup sour cream

2 tablespoons maple syrup

Preheat the oven to 350°F. Line a baking sheet with aluminum foil, and then spray evenly with the cooking spray. Spread the sweet potato in a single layer on the baking sheet and bake for 40 minutes, or until the pieces are slightly browned but not quite fork-tender.

Meanwhile, place a large, heavy soup pot or Dutch oven over medium-high heat and add the oil. Add the prosciutto and cook, stirring frequently, until golden brown. Use a slotted spoon to transfer the prosciutto to paper towels. Do not discard the fat from the pot.

Add the onion, sugar, and cumin and cook over medium heat, stirring frequently, until the onions are tender and golden, about 5 minutes. Stir in the roasted sweet potato, broth, and salt. Bring to a boil, then reduce the heat to low and simmer, covered, stirring occasionally, for 20 minutes.

Add the pears, reduce the heat to very low, and cook until the sweet potato and pears are very tender, about 5 minutes more. Remove from the heat and let cool uncovered for 5 to 10 minutes.

Meanwhile, whisk together the sour cream and maple syrup in a small bowl.

In batches, process the soup mixture in a blender or food processor until very smooth. (Hold the top of the blender firmly with a folded towel to prevent an explosion of hot soup.) Return to a clean soup pot, cover, and keep warm over very low heat until ready to serve. Taste for seasoning.

Ladle the soup into wide, warm bowls and drizzle each one with a little of the maple cream. Scatter with a few strips of prosciutto, and serve immediately.

Two Kinds of Celery Soup

This is a simple and soothing soup for a cool fall day, which boasts a double hit of celery flavor and nutrition. A bonus: the soup is low in calories and the lemon adds a lovely spark.

3 tablespoons extra-virgin olive oil

2 large leeks, white and light green parts, well washed and finely chopped

1 large bunch celery, roughly chopped (about 4 cups), leafy green tops reserved for garnish

1 medium celery root, peeled and roughly chopped (about 4 cups)

1 large russet potato, peeled and finely chopped

2 quarts (8 cups) low-sodium chicken or vegetable broth, homemade (page 230 or 231) or store-bought

2 bay leaves

2 tablespoons fresh lemon juice

½ teaspoon kosher salt

Ground white pepper

2 tablespoons roughly chopped fresh flat-leaf parsley

½ cup grated Asiago cheese

Place a large, heavy soup pot or Dutch oven over medium-low heat and add the oil. Add the leeks and cook, stirring, until softened, about 5 minutes. Add the celery and celery root, increase the heat to medium, and cook, stirring, until the celery releases its aroma, about 4 minutes more.

Add the potato, broth, bay leaves, lemon juice, salt, and pepper to taste. Bring to a boil, then reduce the heat to low and simmer, partially covered, until all the vegetables are tender, 30 to 40 minutes.

Remove from the heat and discard the bay leaves. Taste for seasoning. Roughly chop the reserved celery leaves. Ladle into wide, warm bowls or tall mugs and scatter with the celery leaves, parsley, and cheese.

Winter Favorites

Four generations: Mike, Peter, Chris, and William Wallace at William's Christening. Photo by Craig Paulsen.

Soup-making is an especially satisfying way to spend
winter afternoons, because these hearty mixtures take longer to cook than the quick, cool soups of summer. The mouthwatering smell of the kitchen, with sautéing onions and barely bubbling soups, makes me happy to stay at home and work on various indoor projects. Winter soups usually feature tons of beans and earthy root vegetables, which make for hearty and filling meals to feed your family. In the winter I prepare soups every week and serve them for both lunch and dinner. Leftover soup is a great, economical way to fill up the children's lunch boxes with a warm and nutritious meal.

Instead of cream, I often use pureed vegetables or beans to thicken and add luscious texture to soups like my Baby Lima Bean and Swiss Chard Soup. I remove several cups of the mixture, puree it in a blender, and then stir it back into the soup. I am particularly fond of topping these bean soups with a crisp green vegetable to add a fresh note—this is my signature soup-salad combo.

Tortellini Meatball Soup was always a favorite of our kids for school lunches, because it would keep them warm and satisfied until I arrived to pick them up with a snack. While I adore the heartier soups, I am also happy to serve a lighter, healthy meal: my Hearty Seafood Soup is a colorful and tasty way to get heart-healthy fish into the family's diet. Our children were always happy to see this beautiful soup simmering on the stovetop when they came home at the end of a dark and cold winter afternoon.

Chicken has always been Chris's favorite food, and it remains his "comfort food" of choice on a Saturday night prior to his Sunday morning show. From my childhood, I remember the chicken and dumplings my mother used to make, and after roasting many, many chickens I decided that I'd make a simple, one-pot meal, Chicken Soup and Herb Dumplings. Alongside a field green salad topped with toasted pecans and sliced pears, this is a beautiful menu for our Saturday night.

During the bustle of the Christmas holidays, our house is trimmed and pretty—like a celebration of light—and we like to entertain our family and friends with small dinner parties. My Celery Root and Parsnip Puree is a perfect way to start off a more formal dinner. It's a nice alternative to the starchy potatoes usually served in soups and stews at this time of year, and best of all, you can make it ahead of time. The result: more time to enjoy your guests!

We can't discuss winter in the Wallace household without mentioning football. Our three boys are in a wildly competitive fantasy football league, and on Sunday afternoons this league is taken Very Seriously. They pull out their

above left: "Talk to the hand." Catherine and Sarah on our wedding day. *above right*: Vogueing. Photos by Marty Hublitz.

laptops, check their lineups to see which one has the advantage, and engage in heated brotherly arguments. That's when I'll prepare the Ancho Pork and Hominy Soup, a lighter alternative to chili that still packs plenty of flavor. I like to serve the soup with cornbread muffins, and toss a big caesar salad for the boys. (I prefer a lighter salad, but the boys never seem to get tired of caesar!) I usually make my football Sunday soup ahead of the kickoff so I can sit and enjoy the games with my family instead of fussing around in the kitchen.

Thanksgiving family shot. Andrew, Catherine, Peter, Megan, Remick, Sarah, and Winston.
Photo by Larry Martin.

Baby Lima Bean and Swiss Chard Soup

SERVES 8

Sometimes, baby lima beans—milder in flavor than navy and white beans—make a nice change for our family bean soups. Adding the Swiss chard just at the end of the cooking time, then allowing it to wilt slightly, contributes a "fresh" note to this comforting winter soup.

TIPS

• If you forget to soak the lima beans overnight, use the quick-soak method: Combine the beans and enough cold water to cover them by 2 inches. Bring to a boil over high heat, then remove from the heat and cover the pan. Let stand for 1 to 2 hours, then drain well, and proceed with the recipe.

• Save the stems of the Swiss chard for another use. (Cut crosswise and sizzle in olive oil with a little garlic until tender, for instance.)

• Cooking times for dried beans vary enormously, depending on how old they are; check the beans starting after 45 minutes of cooking time. The beans should be very tender before you puree them.

(recipe continues on page 66)

French Onion Soup

My mother-in-law Kappy Leonard belongs to the Columbia Country Club. Early in Chris's and my courtship (and in fact throughout our life together) she has treated our family to wonderful dinners at the club. Fourteen years ago, she very graciously hosted our prenuptial dinner in a beautiful private dining room.

Chris's daughter Catherine and my daughter Sarah are not just sisters but the best of friends. When the girls were younger and first met, they always ordered French onion soup at the club. This tasty soup still stimulates memories of that time, when they were forming a sisterly and family bond. I think part of the fun of the soup involved their shared tradition of pinching small bits of cheese off each other's bowl of soup!

> **TIPS**
> • French onion soup is traditionally made with beef broth, but our family prefers the lighter flavor of chicken broth. Feel free to substitute a good homemade or low-sodium beef broth, preferably organic.
> • Substitute 4 large leeks, both the white and light green parts, very thinly sliced, for the yellow onion, if desired.

(recipe continues on page 69)

2 tablespoons extra-virgin olive oil

4 large red onions, very thinly sliced

1 large yellow onion, very thinly sliced

¼ teaspoon sugar

2 garlic cloves, minced

2 quarts (8 cups) low-sodium chicken broth, homemade (page 230) or store-bought

½ cup dry white wine

1 bay leaf

½ teaspoon minced fresh thyme or ¼ teaspoon dried

2 teaspoons kosher salt

Freshly ground black pepper

Six ½-inch-thick slices baguette, preferably slightly stale

¾ cup coarsely grated Gruyère cheese

TIPS

• *French onion soup is traditionally made with beef broth, but our family prefers the lighter flavor of chicken broth. Feel free to substitute a good homemade or low-sodium beef broth, preferably organic.*

• *Substitute 4 large leeks, both the white and light green parts, very thinly sliced, for the yellow onion, if desired.*

Place a large nonstick soup pot or Dutch oven over medium-low heat and add the oil. Add the red onions and cook, stirring occasionally, until wilted and softened, about 15 minutes.

Add the yellow onion and sugar and continue cooking, stirring frequently, until the onions are brown and caramelized, 30 to 45 minutes. (Don't leave the kitchen during this time; watch the pot carefully so you don't scorch the onions.) Add the garlic and cook for 1 minute more.

Stir in the broth, wine, bay leaf, thyme, salt, and pepper to taste and bring to a boil. Partially cover the pot, reduce the heat to low, and simmer until the flavors are well blended, about 30 minutes. Taste for seasoning. Discard the bay leaf. (At this point, you could remove from the heat, cover the pot, and let stand for up to 1 hour. Warm through before serving.)

Preheat the broiler to high heat and place the top rack about 6 inches from the heat source.

Ladle the soup into six individual flameproof soup bowls, distributing the onions evenly.

Place 1 slice of bread on top of each bowl and sprinkle with the cheese, dividing it evenly. Place the soup bowls under the broiler and broil until the cheese is bubbly and browned, 3 to 4 minutes. Let stand for 2 minutes (to prevent burning your tongue) and then serve.

Hot-and-Sour Soup

SERVES 8

Our son Remick loves any food that is either hot or sour.
He pours hot sauces from all over the world onto his food every
day, and his favorite potato chip flavor is salt and vinegar.
In this soup, I get to provide both of his favorite flavors together!
This is a hearty, spicy soup that will satisfy any hungry person,
young or old.

TIP
*If you prefer, substitute about 6 ounces fresh
shiitake mushrooms for the dried mushrooms
called for here. There is no need to cook them first
before adding to the soup. Just trim off and discard
the tough stem ends and add with the bamboo
shoots.*

2 ounces dried Chinese black or shiitake mushrooms or a mixture

⅓ cup rice vinegar

1½ tablespoons low-sodium soy sauce

2 teaspoons Asian chile oil

1 teaspoon toasted Asian sesame oil

1 teaspoon freshly ground black pepper

4 tablespoons cornstarch

½ cup water

1½ quarts (6 cups) low-sodium chicken broth, homemade (page 230) or store-bought

1 cup (about 10 ounces, drained) thinly sliced bamboo shoots, rinsed well

2 boneless skinless chicken breasts (about 7 ounces each), sliced crosswise, about ⅓-inch thick

4 to 6 ounces firm tofu, drained and cut into cubes (about ¾ cup)

2 large eggs, well beaten

In a large glass measuring cup, cover the dried mushrooms with boiling water; let soak for 30 minutes. Drain the mushrooms (reserve the soaking water) and slice them thinly. Set aside. Strain the soaking water to remove any grit, and set 1 cup of the water aside.

In a small bowl, stir together the vinegar, soy sauce, chile oil, sesame oil, and pepper. Set aside.

In another small bowl, whisk the cornstarch and water until smooth. Set aside (whisking again to combine just before adding to hot soup).

Place a large, heavy soup pot or Dutch oven over medium-high heat. Add the broth and reserved mushroom soaking liquid; bring to a simmer.

Add the soaked mushrooms and bamboo shoots and simmer until the soup is nicely blended and aromatic, about 5 minutes.

Reduce the heat to medium-low so the soup is just simmering. Add the chicken and tofu and simmer until the chicken is cooked through and firm, about 4 minutes.

Add the soy sauce mixture and the cornstarch mixture to the soup. Return to a simmer and stir occasionally until the soup begins to thicken, about 3 minutes.

Remove the soup from the heat, add the beaten eggs, and immediately whisk with a fork until little shreds of cooked egg form.

Taste for seasoning, and adjust with vinegar, pepper, and/or soy sauce as necessary. Ladle into warm bowls and serve immediately.

Green Kale and Kielbasa Soup

This is a hearty, vitamin-rich soup that will satisfy the meat-and-potato lovers in your family, while also satisfying their nutritional need for fresh green vegetables during the dark days of winter. This tasty soup will stick to your loved ones' bones and make them feel cherished and protected against the cold.

Oxtail Soup

SERVES 8

When I was a teenager, my aunt Lela came over from Norwich, England, to live with my family after her husband, a butcher, passed away. At first she dressed like a nun, and I thought she might be headed for a convent. Then, the lipstick came out and Auntie Lela turned just a little bit wild!

Lela really did understand how to select and prepare the most delicious cuts of meats—a few of her favorites (and ours) were steak and kidney pie, bubble and squeak, and oxtail soup. At first, as a typical teenager, I thought oxtail soup sounded crazy and I wanted nothing to do with it.

Today, this rich and beefy soup is one of my all-time winter favorites!

For a little extra sophistication, stir in ¼ cup of medium-dry sherry just before serving.

3 pounds oxtails, cut about
1 inch thick

Kosher salt and freshly ground
black pepper

¼ cup all-purpose flour
(optional)

2 tablespoons olive oil

1 small onion, finely chopped

2 quarts (8 cups) low-sodium
beef broth, homemade
(page 232) or store-bought

1 sprig fresh thyme

1 large carrot, peeled and
finely chopped

2 stalks celery, finely chopped

¼ cup roughly chopped
fresh parsley

1 bay leaf

1 cup tomato sauce

1 teaspoon fresh lemon juice

1 lemon, cut into eight ¼-inch
slices

Season both sides of each oxtail piece with salt and pepper. If desired, dredge lightly with flour and shake off the excess (see Tip below).

Place a large, heavy soup pot or Dutch oven over medium-high heat and add the oil. In two batches, brown the oxtails for 4 to 5 minutes on each side. Transfer to a plate.

Add the onion to the pot and cook, stirring, until tender, about 5 minutes.

Add the broth, thyme, 1 teaspoon salt, pepper to taste, and then the oxtails. Simmer, partially covered, until the meat comes loose from the bones, about 4 hours.

Transfer the meat to a platter and, when cool enough to handle, remove all the meat from the bones and shred with two forks. Discard the fat, gristle, and bones. Tip the pot to one side and spoon off most of the fat from the top. Return the shredded meat to the soup.

Add the carrot, celery, parsley, bay leaf, and tomato sauce to the soup, and simmer gently, partially covered, until the vegetables are tender, about 1 hour more. Stir in the lemon juice. Discard the bay leaf.

Adjust the seasoning with salt and pepper and ladle into warm bowls. Float a lemon slice in the center of each bowl and serve at once.

TIP

Flouring the oxtails before browning will yield a very thick soup. If you prefer, omit this step. The addition of tomato sauce provides enough thickening action to yield a soup with good richness and body, similar to the consistency of heavy cream.

Mexican Albondigas

SERVES 8

Our family is crazy about Mexican food. The younger kids are big fans of the restaurant chain Chipotle, and some of our happiest times have been spent at a local Mexican restaurant called Cactus Cantina. Mexican cooking offers many great choices for filling up your hungry clan. Here, I love the way the meatballs are baked in the oven and then later added to a savory and colorful Mexican broth.

FOR THE MEATBALLS

Nonstick cooking spray

1 pound boneless skinless chicken breasts or thighs (about 2 breasts or 4 to 5 thighs), cut into ½-inch chunks

1 pound pork tenderloin, cut into ½-inch chunks

1½ cups shredded yellow squash (about 2 small squash)

1 cup roughly chopped fresh cilantro (leaves and tender stems only)

¼ cup raw long-grain white rice

1 large egg

1 teaspoon kosher salt

1 teaspoon freshly ground black pepper

To make the meatballs: Preheat the oven to 400°F. Spray a baking sheet with nonstick spray or use a nonstick baking sheet.

In a large food processor, combine the chicken, pork, squash, cilantro, rice, egg, salt, and pepper. Process for 1 minute, or until evenly blended.

Scoop out some of the mixture and form meatballs by hand, 1 inch in diameter (about the size of a small lime). Place them on the prepared baking sheet as you work; you should have about 20 meatballs.

Bake for 18 minutes, or until firm. Set aside while you make the soup.

(recipe continues on page 80)

FOR THE SOUP

2 tablespoons extra-virgin olive oil

½ small yellow or white onion, roughly chopped

1 small red or green bell pepper, cored, seeded, and finely diced

4 garlic cloves, minced

3 quarts (12 cups) low-sodium chicken broth, homemade (page 230) or store-bought

One 15-ounce can diced tomatoes, drained

One 4-ounce can chopped green chiles, drained

½ cup raw long-grain white rice

1 tablespoon ground cumin

1 tablespoon kosher salt

1 tablespoon freshly ground black pepper, or to taste

1 cup fresh or thawed frozen corn kernels, preferably white

2 small zucchini, halved lengthwise and thinly sliced

2 tablespoons fresh lime juice

FOR SERVING

Lime wedges

Coarsely chopped fresh cilantro

Warm corn tortillas

To make the soup: Place a large, heavy soup pot or Dutch oven over medium heat and add the oil. Add the onion and bell pepper and cook, stirring, until the onion is tender, about 5 minutes. Stir in the garlic and cook, stirring, for 1 minute more.

Add the broth, tomatoes, chiles, rice, cumin, salt, and black pepper and bring to a boil.

With a slotted spoon, lower the meatballs into the boiling soup. As soon as the soup begins to simmer again, reduce the heat to low so it continues to simmer gently. Partially cover and cook for 10 minutes, then add the corn and zucchini and simmer until the rice is cooked, about 25 minutes more.

Remove from the heat and stir in the lime juice. Taste for seasoning and adjust with salt, black pepper, and cumin as desired.

Ladle into warm bowls and serve the lime wedges and cilantro on the side. Pass the warm tortillas at the table.

> **TIPS**
> - *To warm the tortillas, wrap the stack in aluminum foil and place in a 200°F oven for 20 minutes.*
> - *Be sure to use long-grain rice for this soup; short-grain rice will quickly turn starchy and gooey.*
> - *For a colorful and rich garnish, top the soup with 1 or 2 diced avocados.*

Tortellini Meatball Soup

SERVES 8 TO 10

This chunky, hearty Italian-style soup is one of the Wallace family's favorites. It is delicious and satisfying on a cold winter's day. Packed steaming hot into a thermos, it makes a great addition to a kid's lunch box. This soup is simple to prepare and will last for about three days in the refrigerator.

(recipe continues on page 83)

1 pound bulk sweet Italian sausage

⅔ cup fine plain dry breadcrumbs

Kosher salt and freshly ground black pepper

2 tablespoons extra-virgin olive oil

1 medium onion, finely chopped

4 carrots, peeled, quartered lengthwise, and sliced about ⅓-inch thick

6 garlic cloves, minced

2 quarts (8 cups) low-sodium chicken broth, homemade (page 230) or store-bought

1 cup water

Two 9-ounce packages fresh four-cheese tortellini

2 tablespoons Italian seasoning

2 tablespoons chopped fresh basil

2 roasted red peppers from a jar, drained and chopped

2 tablespoons fresh lemon juice

6 cups loosely packed baby spinach leaves, washed and drained

To make the meatballs, combine the sausage and breadcrumbs in a large bowl and add a pinch each of salt and black pepper. With clean hands, mix together and form meatballs about ¾ inch in diameter. Set aside (the meatballs are not precooked).

Place a large, heavy soup pot or Dutch oven over medium heat and add the oil. Add the onion and carrots and cook, stirring, until tender, about 5 minutes. Add the garlic and cook, stirring, for 1 minute more.

Add the broth, water, ¾ teaspoon salt, and black pepper to taste. Bring to a boil.

Add the meatballs and cook for 6 minutes, adjusting the heat so the broth simmers, but doesn't boil furiously. Add the tortellini and Italian seasoning and cook for 4 minutes. Add the basil, roasted peppers, and lemon juice and simmer until the tortellini are tender, about 3 minutes more.

Gently stir in the spinach and remove from the heat. Cover the pot and let stand until the spinach is wilted but still bright green, about 2 minutes. Taste for seasoning.

Ladle into warm bowls and serve.

Pasta and Chickpea Soup

SERVES 6 TO 8

This chunky soup is very Italian in spirit—it's essentially the national winter dish of Italians and non-Italians everywhere: pasta e fagioli.

3 ounces thick-cut pancetta, diced

4 garlic cloves, minced

1 cup diced canned Italian plum tomatoes, drained

Two 15-ounce cans of chickpeas, rinsed and drained

1½ quarts (6 cups) low-sodium chicken broth, homemade (page 230) or store-bought

2 teaspoons kosher salt

Freshly ground black pepper

¾ pound small pasta shapes (macaroni, orzo, or broken-up pieces of spaghetti), cooked al dente (see Tip below)

½ cup grated Pecorino Romano cheese, for garnish

Place a large, heavy soup pot or Dutch oven over medium-high heat and add the pancetta. Cook, stirring frequently, until just crisp, about 5 minutes. Add the garlic and cook until only just beginning to brown, about 2 minutes (don't let it burn!).

Add the tomatoes and cook, stirring, to thicken slightly, 2 to 3 minutes. Add the chickpeas, broth, salt, and pepper to taste. Bring up to a simmer and cook for 5 minutes. Add the cooked pasta, reduce the heat to low, and simmer for 5 minutes more to blend the flavors. Taste for seasoning.

Ladle the soup into warm bowls or tall mugs, and sprinkle with some of the cheese. Serve immediately.

> **TIPS**
> • *Cook the pasta ahead of time, just until al dente, then drain in a colander, return to the cooking pot, and cover with cold water. Let stand until you are ready to add to the soup, then drain again, shaking well to remove excess water.*
> • *To make a vegetarian soup, omit the pancetta here and substitute vegetable broth for the chicken broth. Chickpeas are a wonderful source of protein for vegetarians and meat-eaters alike, and they just happen to be delicious! (If you do not use the pancetta, you will need to add a little more salt— pancetta is very salty.)*

Black-Eyed Pea Soup

SERVES 8

In the South, black-eyed peas are a cherished tradition, believed to bring good luck to those who eat them. For this reason, most Southerners—even today—serve black-eyed peas on New Year's Day.

What a tasty way to fill up your family, and bring them luck as well!

1 tablespoon extra-virgin olive oil

1½ pounds bulk lean pork or turkey sausage

1 medium onion, finely chopped

1 stalk celery, finely chopped

Four 15-ounce cans black-eyed peas, rinsed and drained

2½ cups low-sodium chicken broth, homemade (page 230) or store-bought

One 15-ounce can diced tomatoes, with juice

One 7-ounce can diced green chiles, with juice

2 tablespoons chili powder

1 teaspoon kosher salt

Freshly ground black pepper

Place a large, heavy soup pot or Dutch oven over medium-high heat and add the oil. Add the sausage, onion, and celery, and cook, stirring frequently, until the onion is softened and slightly golden and the sausage no longer pink, about 15 minutes.

Add the black-eyed peas, broth, tomatoes, chiles, and chili powder. Stir to blend and add the salt and pepper to taste.

Bring to a boil, then reduce the heat to low, cover, and simmer for about 45 minutes. Taste for seasoning.

Ladle into warm bowls and serve.

White Bean Soup

Pureeing half of this soup gives it a lovely, rich thickness without adding the calories of cream. I like to use this method of thickening soups because it's a healthy choice, but you'd never know it! The Swiss chard is a wonderful taste- and vitamin-booster for this simple bean soup.

TIPS
• Save the stems from the Swiss chard for another use (they are delicious when sliced about ¼ inch thick and sautéed with a little shallot and butter until tender).
• If you don't have time to soak the beans overnight, use the quick-soak method on page 64.
• When soaking beans overnight, be sure to use a large bowl and cover with at least 2 inches of water; the beans will absorb every bit of it!
• You can make this soup up to 3 days before serving. Cool and refrigerate, well sealed (or freeze for up to 2 months). Remember to taste for seasoning, and adjust as desired, after reheating.

- 2 cups dried Great Northern, cannellini, or baby lima beans, soaked in water to cover overnight
- 2 tablespoons extra-virgin olive oil
- 2 yellow onions, coarsely chopped
- 4 carrots, peeled and coarsely chopped
- 2 small bunches red Swiss chard, thick stems removed, leaves cut crosswise about ¾ inch thick, divided
- 3 quarts (12 cups) low-sodium chicken broth, homemade (page 230) or store-bought
- One 15-ounce can diced tomatoes, drained
- ¼ cup finely chopped fresh basil
- 6 garlic cloves, minced
- 1 teaspoon kosher salt
- Freshly ground black pepper
- ¼ cup roughly chopped fresh flat-leaf parsley
- ¼ cup grated Parmesan or Romano cheese

Drain the beans well and pick over to remove any discolored beans or debris.

Place a large, heavy soup pot or Dutch oven over medium heat and add the oil. Add the onions and cook, stirring occasionally, until softened, about 5 minutes. Add the carrots and cook, stirring, until softened, about 3 minutes more. Add half of the Swiss chard and stir until just wilted, 2 to 3 minutes.

Add the broth, beans, tomatoes, basil, and garlic. Bring to a boil, then reduce the heat to low and simmer, partially covered, until the beans are tender, 1 to 1¼ hours. Remove from the heat and let cool for 5 to 10 minutes.

Scoop out about half of the soup and transfer to a blender or food processor, and process until smooth. (Hold the top of the blender firmly with a folded towel to prevent an explosion of hot soup.) Return to the pot and place over medium-low heat to warm through.

Add the remaining Swiss chard and cook until the chard is wilted but still green, about 3 minutes. Stir in the salt, pepper to taste, and two-thirds of the parsley. Taste for seasoning.

Ladle the soup into warm bowls and garnish with the remaining parsley and the cheese.

Hearty Seafood Soup

SERVES 10

We love seafood and eat it frequently to make sure we get plenty of heart-healthy Omega-3 fish oils into our diet. Now that Chris and I are empty-nesters, eating fish more often is part of our healthy routine. This hearty soup features chorizo sausage and a tomato base that adds body and flavor. For a more substantial supper, serve over a mound of mashed potatoes or rice. You may not need any salt at all here; the flavors are clean and simple, and perfect as they are!

(recipe continues on page 92)

2 tablespoons extra-virgin olive oil

1¼ pounds fresh chorizo sausage links

2 fennel bulbs, quartered, cored, and thinly sliced crosswise (reserve the feathery fronds, if still attached)

1 large yellow onion, thinly sliced

1½ quarts (6 cups) seafood broth

One 28-ounce can crushed tomatoes

Zest of 1 scrubbed orange, cut into thick strips (see Tip below)

Freshly ground black pepper

2 pounds firm white-fleshed fish fillets, such as halibut, cut into 1½-inch pieces

2 pounds medium shrimp, peeled and deveined

2 pounds clams or mussels, well scrubbed

Kosher salt (optional)

Place a large, heavy soup pot or Dutch oven over medium heat and add the oil. Add the sausage and cook, turning occasionally, until browned, about 8 minutes.

Remove the sausage and set aside to cool.

Add the fennel and onion to the pot and cook, stirring occasionally, until tender, about 10 minutes.

Cut the sausage into 1-inch lengths and return it to the pot. Add the broth, tomatoes, orange zest, and pepper to taste. Bring to a boil, then reduce the heat to low and simmer for about 10 minutes, to blend the flavors.

Add the fish, stir gently, cover, and cook for 3 minutes. Add the shrimp and clams; stir them gently into the soup and cover the pot. Cook until the shrimp are opaque and the clams open, 5 to 6 minutes. Discard any clams that have not opened after 7 minutes. Taste for seasoning and add salt, if desired (see headnote on page 90).

Ladle the chunky soup into warm bowls, distributing all the ingredients evenly. Garnish with the reserved fennel fronds and serve immediately.

TIPS
• *Before removing the peel, or zest, of any citrus fruit—such as oranges, lemons, or limes—scrub the fruit under hot running water; this will remove any wax that may have been used to keep it blemish-free during transport.*
• *Use a vegetable peeler to remove the orange zest in strips (use either navel or Valencia oranges). Be sure to leave behind as much of the bitter white pith as possible, removing only a thin strip of bright orange zest.*
• *Preferably, choose a wild-caught, sustainable species of fish.*

Irish Stew

SERVES 4 TO 6

After my first marriage ended, a wonderful young woman came into my life: Dolores Dixon (now Dolores Perkins), and she is still a dear friend of our family. I was a single mother of two, and Dolores helped me run our lives.

As a proud Irishwoman, this was her go-to dinner when we were all busy. This famous stew is not browned, and I have no idea if the recipe is authentic or not. (I like to call it the dump-'n'-stir method!) No matter, because it is part of our family tradition: tried, true, and enjoyed over many years, just like our continuing friendship with Dolores and now her husband, Ray!

(recipe continues on page 95)

1½ pounds white rose (boiling) potatoes, peeled and thinly sliced

2 pounds lamb (from the leg or shoulder), cut into 1½-inch pieces

1 small yellow onion, thinly sliced

Kosher salt and freshly ground black pepper

3 cups low-sodium beef broth, warm (see Tip below)

2 tablespoons finely chopped fresh parsley

In a large, heavy soup pot or Dutch oven, layer one-quarter of the potatoes, one-third of the lamb, and a few slices of onion. Season with salt and pepper (you will use a total of about 1½ teaspoons salt). Repeat the layering twice, ending with a final layer of potatoes on top.

Pour the broth around the edges of the pot, so it doesn't wash the seasonings to the bottom. Scatter with the parsley.

Bring to a boil, then reduce the heat, cover the pot, and simmer gently over very low heat until everything is tender, about 2½ hours (see Tip below); shake the pot occasionally, to keep the potatoes from sticking. When done, the potatoes and the lamb should be very tender, and the onions melted away.

Using a large spoon, divide among warm bowls and serve.

> **TIPS**
> • *Warm the beef broth in the microwave.*
> • *When you simmer a liquid mixture for a long period of time, you will have to gradually reduce the heat, bit by bit, to avoid letting the mixture boil furiously. For this reason, you'll need to check the pot occasionally.*

Pot-au-Feu Soup

SERVES 6 TO 8

Pot-au-feu is a simple, no-fuss French beef stew that uses large pieces of beef, rather than the smaller chunks we tend to serve in the U.S. It is homey and restorative and has been popular in the French countryside for hundreds of years. I like to serve this dish with a little more broth, thus transforming it from a stew into a soup. The beef marrowbone adds a wonderful richness, and is a must for this famous winter warmer-upper.

- 1 bouquet garni (see Tip below)
- 3 pounds chuck roast, excess fat trimmed away, cut into 6 pieces
- 1 beef marrowbone, in one piece or sawed into several pieces
- 3 cups low-sodium beef broth, homemade (page 232) or store-bought
- 3 cups water
- 1 yellow onion, cut into large chunks
- 1 pound carrots, peeled and cut into large chunks
- 1 pound white rose (boiling) potatoes, peeled and quartered
- 1½ teaspoons kosher salt
- Freshly ground black pepper
- ½ pound turnips, peeled and cut into large chunks
- ½ pound white or green cabbage, coarsely chopped
- Prepared horseradish and Dijon mustard, for serving

Place the bouquet garni in a large, heavy soup pot or Dutch oven. Add the chuck roast, marrowbone, broth, water, and onion. Bring to a boil, then reduce the heat to low, cover, and simmer for 30 minutes, skimming off any foam that rises to the surface. Continue simmering very gently for 2 hours more.

Add the carrots, potatoes, salt, and pepper to taste. Cover and cook for 30 minutes, then add the turnips and cook, covered, for 15 minutes more. Add the cabbage and cook, again covered, until tender, 10 to 15 minutes.

Remove the marrowbone(s) and, if there is any marrow remaining in the center, scoop it out and add to the soup pot. Discard the marrowbones. Discard the bouquet garni and taste for seasoning.

Divide the beef among warmed bowls and top with the vegetables and broth. Serve with horseradish and mustard on the side.

TIP
To make a bouquet garni, place 2 sprigs of fresh flat-leaf parsley, 2 sprigs of fresh thyme, and 1 bay leaf on a square of cheesecloth. Bring up the corners and tie securely with kitchen twine. This way, the flavors will permeate the soup, and the bouquet garni can be easily removed before serving time.

Chicken Soup and Herb Dumplings

SERVES 6

This dish starts off as a basic chicken soup, but when you add the herb dumplings it becomes a hearty winter meal, perfect for either lunch or dinner. Chris loves chicken—in fact, chicken is the only dinner he'll have on Saturday nights before his Sunday morning show! It is safe to say that chicken is his comfort food (and that he is a tad superstitious). Sometimes when it is cold out and I am tired of making roasted chicken, this is my winter Saturday night dinner of choice—Chris says it still counts as an "official" chicken dinner!

(recipe continues on page 100)

I like to make dropped dumplings for this soup, but you can also make smaller dumplings.
Roll the dumpling dough out (on a well-floured flour surface) to about ¼ inch thick, then cut into squares or even smaller, triangular dumplings. Use a pizza knife to cut the dough if you like. Adjust the cooking time as necessary for the smaller dumplings.

Bring the soup to a very gentle simmer. Working quickly and using two spoons, form 12 dumplings of about 1 tablespoon each and drop them into the broth. Immediately cover the pot and cook at a very gentle simmer for 7 to 10 minutes (do not let the soup boil), until the dumplings are firm.

Ladle into warm bowls and serve, distributing the dumplings, chicken, and vegetables evenly.

Using two tablespoons, scoop up about 1 tablespoon of the dumpling mixture.

With one of the tablespoons, push the dumpling toward the point of the other spoon.

Holding the spoons just above the surface of the soup, scoop off and let the dumpling drop into the soup. Repeat to make about 12 dumplings.

Cover and simmer until all the dumplings are puffy.

Celery Root and Parsnip Puree

SERVES 6

Root vegetables such as celery root and parsnips make for a wonderful, less starchy substitute for potatoes in pot pies, stews, and soups. We like to serve this delicate soup as the elegant start to a holiday meal.

TIPS
• Pureeing a piping hot soup in a blender can be dangerous! Hot liquids will expand and blow the lid right off the blender, spraying hot soup everywhere. To be safe, always let the soup cool for 5 to 10 minutes before blending. Never fill the blender more than half full (blend in batches) and always hold the top firmly with a folded towel. If necessary, transfer the soup back to a clean pot, and warm through before serving.
• You can make this puree 2 days before serving to guests or as a family meal; just reheat on low and adjust the seasoning prior to serving time.

3 tablespoons butter

2 large leeks, white and light green parts only, well washed and roughly chopped

1 large celery root (about 12 ounces), peeled, quartered, and cut into ¾-inch chunks

3 medium parsnips, peeled and roughly chopped

1½ quarts (6 cups) low-sodium chicken or vegetable broth, homemade (page 230 or 231) or store-bought

Kosher salt and freshly ground black pepper

Grated zest of 1 scrubbed orange, for garnish

Pinch of freshly grated nutmeg

In a large, heavy soup pot or Dutch oven, melt the butter over medium-low heat. Add the leeks and cook, stirring occasionally, until slightly softened, about 4 minutes.

Add the celery root and parsnips, and cook, stirring occasionally, for 5 minutes more. Add the broth, increase the heat and bring to a simmer. Partially cover the pot and cook until the vegetables are quite tender, about 20 minutes. Remove from the heat and let stand, uncovered, for 10 minutes.

In batches, puree in a blender or food processor, or use a handheld immersion blender. (If using a traditional blender, hold the top of the blender firmly with a folded towel to prevent an explosion of hot soup.)

Warm the soup through over medium-low heat and season with salt and pepper to taste.

Ladle into warm bowls and sprinkle with a little orange zest and nutmeg.

VARIATION
Instead of the orange and nutmeg garnish, drizzle with a few drops of truffle oil (a little goes a long way!) or best-quality extra-virgin olive oil. Top with a pinch of finely chopped fresh flat-leaf parsley or snipped fresh chives.

Ancho Pork and Hominy Soup

This very satisfying winter soup is hearty, yet a lighter alternative to chili for game days. It is a one-pot meal for cold blustery days and makes your house smell wonderful! Adding the hominy, in addition to corn, really makes this chunky, pretty soup taste like summer. If you make this soup when corn is in season, by all means substitute 2 cups of fresh corn kernels (from about 4 ears) for the frozen corn.

(recipe continues on page 106)

2½ tablespoons ancho chile powder

2½ teaspoons dried oregano

2 teaspoons smoked paprika

1½ teaspoons ground cumin

1 teaspoon kosher salt

2 pounds pork tenderloin, trimmed and cut into ¾-inch pieces

3 tablespoons extra-virgin olive oil, divided

1 large yellow onion, finely chopped

2 small green bell peppers, cored, seeded, and finely chopped

4 to 5 garlic cloves, minced

2 quarts (8 cups) low-sodium chicken broth, homemade (page 230) or store-bought

Three 15-ounce cans white hominy, drained

One 28-ounce can fire-roasted diced tomatoes, with juice

One 16-ounce bag frozen sweet corn, thawed

Tortilla chips or Jalapeño Cornbread Muffins (recipe opposite), for serving

In a large bowl, combine the ancho chile powder, oregano, paprika, cumin, and salt. Set 1½ teaspoons of the spice mixture aside and add the pork to the remaining spice mixture. Toss to coat well and let stand for 15 minutes.

Place a large, heavy soup pot or Dutch oven over medium-high heat and add 2 tablespoons of the oil. Add the seasoned pork and cook, stirring occasionally, until browned, about 5 minutes. Remove the pork from the pot and set aside.

Add the remaining tablespoon of oil to the pot and reduce the heat to medium-low; add the onion and bell peppers and cook, stirring occasionally, until tender, 6 to 8 minutes. Add the garlic and cook, stirring, for 1 minute more. (If the spices stick to the pot, add a little of the broth to help deglaze the spices.)

Return the pork to the pan and stir in the reserved spice mixture, broth, hominy, tomatoes, and corn. Bring the soup to a boil, then reduce the heat and simmer gently, uncovered, until nice and thick, about 45 minutes.

Serve with tortilla chips or Jalapeño Cornbread Muffins.

NOTE

Hominy is dried maize that has been soaked in lye, and is popular in Mexican dishes such as menudo and in the deep South, where it's often dried and ground to produce "hominy grits," similar to cornmeal or polenta.

JALAPEÑO CORNBREAD MUFFINS

MAKES 12 MUFFINS

1 cup medium-ground yellow cornmeal

1 cup all-purpose flour

2 tablespoons sugar

2 teaspoons baking powder

1 teaspoon kosher salt

½ teaspoon freshly ground black pepper

¼ teaspoon cayenne pepper

1 large egg, lightly beaten

1 cup buttermilk

6 tablespoons (¾ stick) butter, melted

1 cup fresh corn kernels (from about 2 ears) or thawed frozen corn

2 to 3 jalapeño chiles, or to taste, stemmed, seeded, and minced

Preheat the oven to 425°F and grease a 12-cup muffin pan.

In a large bowl, combine the cornmeal, flour, sugar, baking powder, salt, black pepper, and cayenne. Make a well in the center of the dry mixture and add the egg, buttermilk, butter, corn, and jalapeños. Whisking from the center, combine the ingredients into a loose and slightly lumpy batter.

Pour the batter into the prepared muffin cups and bake for 15 minutes, or until the muffins begin to pull away from the sides of the pan.

Cool the pan on a wire rack for about 10 minutes. Serve warm or at room temperature.

Spring
Favorites

Remick off to the Easter Egg Hunt.

Gathering (and dropping) Easter Eggs.

As spring approaches and the days get warmer and longer, the nation's capital is truly glorious! Washington's famously beautiful cherry trees are in full bloom on the Mall, and the parkway is lined with huge swaths of the daffodils Lady Bird Johnson planted decades ago. As everyone comes out of winter hibernation, the social calendar heats up, too, and there are plenty of activities with friends and family.

As you might imagine, the soups I make in the warmer weather are often lighter in texture and aromatic with the flavor of fresh vegetables. As we cast off our winter sweaters and parkas, we crave soups like my signature Italian Spinach Salad Soup. This warm, pureed soup features a crisp watercress and spinach salad on top, transforming it from simply soup to a healthy and satisfying light meal.

Spring is also baseball season, a sport two of our sons, Andrew and Remick, played for their schools. I usually made a pot of soup earlier in the day, so that when we returned home from watching them swing for the fences, there was a warming and tasty soup ready to eat. There is a three-year age difference between Andrew and Remick, and it was always a thrill to see them play at each other's schools. Chris and I never knew which bench to sit on, so we would pace back and forth between the two. When our youngest son, Remick, was a freshman, he was the starting pitcher—twice!—and had to face Andrew, who was then a senior, at bat. They both had their highs and lows during the game, striking out and hitting home runs off each other. Salmon Chowder was my go-to dish for feeding these hungry gamers because it is hearty yet light, with celery root, lemon, and dill adding a fresh, spring flavor.

Our daughters were extremely involved in their after-school activities, too! In the spring, Sarah had musical rehearsals and often performed late into the nights and on weekends. Catherine, who was on the varsity track team, was always on the run, both literally and figuratively. Young ladies like a light yet filling meal, so I often served my girls one of their favorite spring soups, Chicken Garlic Straciatella, which adds lots of garlic and protein to this old-fashioned Italian favorite.

From the get-go, Easter has been a big tradition in the Wallace household. First, we'd celebrate with a lunch after attending mass. At Granny's house, lunch was accompanied by an Easter egg hunt, which included plastic eggs holding money! I got into the action, dying eggs with the children. I would secretly spirit away some of the kids' favorite dyed eggs, then write their names on each egg with a silver or gold marker. These pretty eggs would become their surprise place

cards at the Easter table. Later in the day, we sat down to an early evening dinner, which usually began with my gorgeous Easter Zucchini-Mint Soup. It's simple to prepare the day before your spring celebration, then gently rewarm and serve in pretty glass bowls. This bright and lively soup is the perfect opener for a classic spring feast of lamb, au gratin potatoes, and asparagus.

Chantima Suka (a.k.a., Jim) cooking in our kitchen.
Photo by Michael Kress.

Me with pea-loving son Remick.

Split Pea Soup

SERVES 6

There is an ongoing dispute in our house as to whether split pea soup is a winter or a spring soup. I like to serve this classic soup when winter is drawing to a close and spring days are calling. The crumbled bacon adds a flavorful counterpoint to the creamy soup. If you serve a ham for Easter, keep the stripped-down ham bone in the freezer until you are ready to make pea soup; cook the bone with the peas, and serve any remaining ham still attached to the bone as a tasty garnish.

(recipe continues on page 112)

1 tablespoon extra-virgin olive oil

1 yellow onion, finely chopped

1 stalk celery, thinly sliced

2 carrots, peeled and thinly sliced

1¼ quarts (5 cups) low-sodium chicken or vegetable broth, homemade (page 230 or 231) or store-bought

1 smoked ham hock

1 cup dried green split peas, rinsed and picked over

2 tablespoons finely chopped fresh flat-leaf parsley

½ teaspoon finely chopped fresh marjoram or ¼ teaspoon dried

2 sprigs fresh thyme

Freshly ground black pepper and kosher salt, to taste

6 slices cooked bacon, crumbled, for garnish (optional)

Place a large, heavy soup pot or Dutch oven over medium-low heat and add the oil Add the onion and cook, stirring occasionally, until softened, about 5 minutes. Add the celery and carrots and continue cooking, again stirring occasionally, until just slightly softened, 3 minutes more.

Add the broth, ham hock, peas, parsley, marjoram, and thyme. Bring to a boil, then reduce the heat to low and simmer, partially covered, until the peas are tender, about 1 hour. Discard the thyme and remove the ham hock (save for another use, if desired; see Tip below).

Let cool for 5 to 10 minutes, then transfer about 2 cups of the soup to a food processor or blender. Process until still slightly chunky, then return the puree to the soup in the pot. (Hold the top of the blender firmly with a folded towel to prevent an explosion of hot soup.)

Over medium heat, return to a simmer and cook until warmed through, about 5 minutes. Season with pepper to taste, then taste for salt; the soup may not need any, since the ham hock is very salty.

Ladle the soup into wide, warm bowls or mugs and garnish with the crumbled bacon (if using).

TIP

The approximate 1 hour of cooking time required to soften most split peas is not enough to fully cook the meat on the ham hock. You can either rinse and reserve it for another use, or, if you'd like to add the ham meat to the soup, simmer the hock in water to cover for about 1½ hours before you begin making the soup.

Minted Sweet Pea and Spinach Soup

SERVES 4 TO 6

Peas are my son Remick's very favorite vegetable, so naturally I created a spring soup that would satisfy his craving for them. Baseball season begins in the early spring, and here's a great way to harvest the season's new peas and mint in a warm meal for your athlete. I love to serve this bright soup after a good game on a crisp afternoon.

3 tablespoons butter

2 tablespoons extra-virgin olive oil

1 large yellow onion, finely chopped

1¼ quarts (5 cups) low-sodium chicken broth, homemade (page 230) or store-bought

15 ounces thawed frozen chopped spinach, squeezed dry

15 ounces thawed frozen peas (see Tip below)

1½ cups fresh mint leaves

1½ cups heavy cream

½ teaspoon kosher salt

Freshly ground black pepper

In a large, heavy soup pot or Dutch oven, melt the butter with the oil over low heat.

Add the onion, cover, and cook, stirring occasionally, until tender and slightly browned, about 25 minutes.

Add the broth, spinach, and peas; bring to a boil, then reduce the heat to low and cook for 4 minutes. Add all but 8 to 12 leaves of mint, reserving the extra for garnish, and simmer for 5 minutes more.

Pour the soup through a fine-meshed strainer, reserving the broth. Transfer the solids to a food processor or blender and add 1 cup of the strained broth. Process until very smooth and return the pureed mixture to the clean pot.

Stir in the heavy cream, salt, pepper to taste, and the remaining strained broth. Return to a simmer over medium-low heat and taste for seasoning.

Ladle into warm bowls or mugs and garnish each with mint leaves.

TIP
If fresh peas are available, by all means use them for this soup! Shell enough peas to yield 2 cups, then blanch in lightly salted boiling water for 2 minutes, drain well, and run under cold running water to stop the cooking and preserve the bright green color.

Chicken Garlic Straciatella

SERVES 4 TO 6

As the winter weather starts to thaw but the days are still chilly and gray, I like to make the transition to the new season with lighter soups that still have enough body and warmth to get our family through the day. Here, I tried adding lots of garlic—what could be wrong with that?— to an old-fashioned Italian favorite. This spring soup hits the spot perfectly!

1¾ quarts (7 cups) low-sodium chicken broth, homemade (page 230) or store-bought

20 garlic cloves, thinly sliced

1 pound boneless skinless chicken tenders, cut into ¾-inch cubes

1 large carrot, peeled and cut into matchstick strips

½ teaspoon kosher salt

Freshly ground black pepper

1 pound baby spinach leaves, slivered

2 tablespoons finely chopped fresh flat-leaf parsley

3 tablespoons grated Pecorino cheese

3 large eggs, lightly beaten

Place a large, heavy soup pot or Dutch oven over medium heat and add the broth and garlic. Bring to a boil, then reduce the heat to low and simmer for 15 minutes. Remove from the heat and let cool for 5 minutes. In a blender or food processor, process the soup (in batches if necessary) until smooth. (Hold the top of the blender firmly with a folded towel to prevent an explosion of hot soup.)

Return the soup to the pot and add the chicken, carrot, salt, and pepper to taste. Bring to a boil, then remove from the heat, cover the pot, and let stand for 10 minutes (this will gently cook the chicken).

Return to medium-low heat and add the spinach, parsley, and cheese. Simmer until the spinach is just wilted but still bright green, about 1 minute. Remove from the heat.

Slowly pour the beaten eggs into the warm soup, stirring with a fork just until threads of cooked egg form. Taste for seasoning. Ladle into wide, warm bowls and serve.

Italian Spinach Salad Soup

SERVES 6 TO 8

This warm, pureed soup has a crisp spinach and watercress salad on the top for appealing crunch, flavor, and color. The richness and body in this soup come from russet potatoes, and it holds up well to support my Italian salad mixture, with cherry tomatoes and Parmesan. This is one of my signature "salad soups" that our family loves when spring is in the air. It is light, and will appeal to the dieters in your family, yet it's full of nutrients and vitamins. For a beautiful presentation at the start of a spring celebration, serve in a pretty soup tureen.

FOR THE SOUP

4 tablespoons (½ stick) butter

1 large onion, chopped

8 garlic cloves, finely chopped

2 tablespoons Italian seasoning

2 quarts (8 cups) low-sodium chicken broth, homemade (page 230) or store-bought

2 large russet potatoes, peeled and chopped

Two 9-ounce boxes frozen chopped spinach, thawed and squeezed dry

½ cup half-and-half (optional)

½ teaspoon kosher salt

Freshly ground black pepper

FOR THE SALAD

3 tablespoons extra-virgin olive oil

1 tablespoon fresh lemon juice

¼ teaspoon kosher salt

Freshly ground black pepper

2 cups loosely packed fresh baby spinach leaves (about 2 ounces)

2 cups loosely packed watercress (leaves and tender stems only)

8 small cherry tomatoes, halved

4 ounces Parmesan cheese, shaved with a vegetable peeler

To make the soup: Place a large, heavy soup pot or Dutch oven over medium heat and add the butter. When it has melted, add the onion, garlic, and Italian seasoning and cook, stirring occasionally, until the onion is tender, about 5 minutes.

Add the broth and potatoes and bring to a boil. Simmer for 5 minutes, then add the spinach, stir, and return to a simmer. Cook for 5 minutes more. Remove from the heat and let cool for about 10 minutes.

In batches, puree soup in a blender or food processor. (Hold the top of the blender firmly with a folded towel to prevent an explosion of hot soup.) Return to the pot.

Stir in the half-and-half (if using), salt, and pepper to taste.

Warm over low heat until hot and taste for seasoning.

To make the salad: In a large bowl, whisk together the oil, lemon juice, salt, and a little pepper. Add the spinach and watercress and toss until evenly coated.

Ladle the soup into warm bowls. Top with some of the salad, a few cherry tomatoes, and the shaved cheese. Serve immediately.

Carrot Soup with Herb Puree

This recipe was slightly adapted from a recipe by David Hagedorn that first appeared in the Washington Post

SERVES 8

Nothing says April like long, thin carrots with their leafy green tops! I can just imagine the Easter bunny hopping though the garden, munching away. I love to serve this soup on a Sunday with an interesting grilled panini, perhaps smoked mozzarella and portobello mushrooms with a smidgen of French mustard.

FOR THE SOUP

2 quarts (8 cups) low-sodium vegetable broth, homemade (page 231) or store-bought

1 pound tender spring carrots with leafy tops, peeled and coarsely chopped (reserve tops for puree below)

1 cup diced mango

1 medium russet potato, peeled and cut into 1-inch cubes

½ cup sugar

2 teaspoons kosher salt

½ teaspoon freshly ground black pepper

FOR THE PUREE

1 cup chopped carrot greens

1 cup loosely packed baby spinach leaves

1 bunch scallions, dark green parts only, roughly chopped (reserve white and light green parts for another use)

1 small bunch fresh dill, coarsely chopped

¼ cup extra-virgin olive oil

1 teaspoon kosher salt

Freshly ground back pepper

½ cup crème fraîche, for garnish

To make the soup: In a large, heavy soup pot or Dutch oven, combine the broth, carrots, mango, potato, sugar, salt, and pepper. Bring to a boil, then reduce the heat to low and simmer until the vegetables are softened, about 20 minutes.

Remove from the heat and let cool for about 10 minutes.

Working in batches, puree the soup in a blender or food processor until smooth. (Hold the top of the blender firmly with a folded towel to prevent an explosion of hot soup.) Return to a clean pot and set aside while you make the puree.

To make the puree: Bring a large pot three-fourths filled with water to a boil. Remove from the heat and immediately add the carrot greens, spinach, scallions, and dill. Stir just until wilted, then immediately drain in a colander and run under cold water to completely stop the cooking process and maintain the bright green color.

Squeeze as much water as possible from the greens, and then place in a food processor along with the oil, salt, and pepper to taste. Process until smooth, about 30 seconds.

Warm the carrot soup over medium-low heat. Spoon some of the puree into warm bowls and ladle soup over the top. Garnish with a dollop of crème fraîche and serve immediately.

Broccolini–Spring Onion Soup

SERVES 4 TO 6

In recent years, broccoli has shared shelf space with two other similarly named vegetables, Broccolini and broccoli raab. Broccolini is a hybrid of broccoli, appearing as small florets atop long, thin stems, all of which are edible except the largest, toughest stem ends. (Broccoli raab is actually a relative of the cabbage.) In spring, Broccolini is a robust but sweet substitute for our standard broccoli. When you combine it with spring onions, the resulting emerald-green, nourishing soup fairly shouts, "Spring is here!"

(recipe continues on page 124)

2 tablespoons extra-virgin olive oil

10 whole scallions, ends trimmed and finely chopped

1½ pounds Broccolini, florets and stalks cut into 1-inch pieces

1½ quarts (6 cups) low-sodium chicken or vegetable broth, homemade (page 230 or 231) or store-bought

½ teaspoon kosher salt

Freshly ground black pepper

½ cup sour cream or plain yogurt, for garnish

Croutons, for garnish

2 tablespoons snipped fresh chives, for garnish

Place a large, heavy soup pot or Dutch oven over medium-low heat and add the oil. When the oil is warm, add the scallions and cook, stirring occasionally, until softened, about 4 minutes. Add the Broccolini and cook, stirring occasionally, until it begins to soften, about 2 minutes more.

Add the broth, salt, and pepper to taste. Bring to a boil, then reduce the heat to low and simmer, partially covered, until the Broccolini is only just tender and still bright green, 15 to 18 minutes.

Remove from the heat and let cool, uncovered, for about 5 minutes.

In batches, puree the soup in a blender or food processor. (Hold the top of the blender firmly with a folded towel to prevent an explosion of hot soup.) Return to the soup to a clean pot and warm through gently over medium heat. Taste for seasoning.

Ladle into warm bowls or tall mugs and garnish with a big dollop of sour cream, a few croutons, and the chives.

Salmon Chowder

SERVES 6

Wild salmon is abundant in the spring, as the rivers start to thaw and the fish start to swim upstream to their spawning grounds. This pretty dish has all the ingredients of a heartier chowder, but the celery root, lemon, and dill give it a fresh spring taste. If you want to dress this chowder up for a spring dinner, bake six disks of puff pastry and place one on top of each bowl just prior to serving. Toss a spring salad and presto: you've created a simply elegant spring supper!

(recipe continues on page 127)

4 ounces thick-sliced bacon, cut into ¼-inch dice

1 medium yellow onion, finely chopped

1½ pounds celery root (about 2 medium celery roots), peeled and cut into ¼-inch dice

3 cups seafood broth or three 8-ounce bottles clam juice

3 cups water

½ pound tiny new potatoes, scrubbed and halved

2 pounds skinless salmon fillet (preferably wild-caught), cut into 1-inch chunks

1½ cups heavy cream

3 tablespoons butter, softened

3 tablespoons all-purpose flour

3 tablespoons finely chopped fresh dill

2 tablespoons finely chopped fresh flat-leaf parsley

1 teaspoon finely grated zest from a scrubbed and dried lemon

2 tablespoons fresh lemon juice

¼ teaspoon kosher salt

Ground white pepper

In a large skillet, cook the bacon over low heat until crisp; transfer to a paper towel–lined plate and pour off all but 2 tablespoons of the fat from the skillet.

Add the onion to the skillet and cook, stirring, until softened, about 3 minutes. Add the celery root, cover the skillet, and cook, stirring occasionally, until tender, about 15 minutes. Set the skillet aside.

In a large, heavy saucepan, combine the broth and water. Bring to a boil and add the potatoes. Simmer until the potatoes are tender, 8 to 10 minutes. Remove potatoes with a slotted spoon and transfer to a platter.

Add the salmon to the saucepan, reduce the heat to low, and simmer gently for about 4 minutes, just until firm; transfer the salmon to the platter with the potatoes.

Add the cream to the saucepan and simmer over medium-low heat, stirring frequently, until reduced by about one-quarter, 15 to 20 minutes (don't let it boil over!).

In a small bowl, use a fork to blend the butter and flour into a smooth paste. Whisk the flour paste into the simmering soup a little at a time, and keep simmering until the soup is smooth and slightly thickened. Keep cooking and stirring for about 3 minutes more, to cook off the taste of the flour.

Add the reserved celery root mixture, potatoes, and salmon. Bring to a gentle simmer and cook for about 2 minutes more, just to warm through. Stir in the dill, parsley, lemon zest and lemon juice, salt, and pepper to taste.

Ladle into warm bowls and scatter with a little of the cooked bacon.

Greek Lemon Soup

On chilly spring days, I like to serve this pretty, traditional Greek soup in wide shallow bowls for four to six guests. I provide crisp pita chips, hummus, and salty Greek olives, to make a rustic lunch or a first course for a more substantial dinner.

When the warmer weather comes along, this soup is elegant and beautiful when served chilled—in slightly smaller portions, to serve eight—in delicate stemless wineglasses. I often float a very thin slice of lemon on top of each, then line them up on a gleaming silver or chrome platter for help-yourself casual events.

1½ quarts (6 cups) low-sodium chicken broth, homemade (page 230) or store-bought

½ cup long-grain rice

3 large egg yolks, preferably from free-range or Omega-3 eggs

¼ cup fresh lemon juice

½ teaspoon kosher salt

Ground white pepper

1 lemon, thinly sliced, for garnish (optional)

About 2 tablespoons finely chopped fresh flat-leaf parsley

Place a large, heavy soup pot or Dutch oven over medium-high heat and add the broth. Bring to a boil, add the rice, and reduce the heat to low so the broth simmers gently. Partially cover and cook, stirring occasionally until the rice is very soft, almost falling apart, about 45 minutes. When the rice is done, remove the soup from the heat.

Whisk the egg yolks and lemon juice together in a medium bowl until smooth. Scoop out about 1 cup of the hot broth, and, whisking all the time, gradually pour into the egg-lemon mixture in a thin stream.

Whisk this mixture back into the remaining soup and return the pot to medium-low heat. Cook, stirring constantly until the soup is just steaming. Do not let the soup come to a boil, or the eggs will curdle! Stir in the salt and pepper to taste. Taste for seasoning.

Serve immediately, or cool to room temperature, then cover and refrigerate for at least 3 hours, or until chilled. Ladle into wide, warm bowls and garnish each one with a lemon slice and a pinch of chopped parsley. If serving cold: ladle carefully—to avoid splashes—into stemmed or stemless wineglasses and garnish as above.

TIP
If serving cold, correct the seasoning just before serving; cold mixtures require more assertive seasoning.

Easter Zucchini-Mint Soup

SERVES 6 TO 8

I like to serve this light soup for the beginning of our Easter meal. It's popular with every member of the family, and looks so pretty in my clear soup bowls, waiting for our family to sit down to a feast of roasted lamb, plus all the favorite spring trimmings, like asparagus and au gratin potatoes.

2 tablespoons extra-virgin olive oil

1 tablespoon butter

1 large leek, white and light green parts only, finely chopped

3 garlic cloves, finely chopped

6 medium zucchini (about 3 pounds), thinly sliced

1¼ quarts (5 cups) low-sodium vegetable broth, homemade (page 231) or store-bought

¾ teaspoon kosher salt

½ teaspoon ground white pepper

1 cup mascarpone

3 tablespoons finely chopped fresh mint, divided

In a large, heavy soup pot or Dutch oven, warm the oil and butter over medium heat. Add the leek and cook, stirring frequently, until slightly softened, about 3 minutes. Add the garlic and cook for 1 minute more.

Add the zucchini and cook until the edges turn bright green, about 3 minutes.

Add the broth, salt, and pepper. Bring to a boil, then reduce the heat to low and simmer, partially covered, until zucchini is tender, about 12 minutes. Let the soup cool uncovered for about 5 minutes.

In batches, puree the soup in a blender or food processor. (Hold the top of the blender firmly with a folded towel to prevent an explosion of hot soup.) Return the pureed soup to a clean pot.

Stir in ¾ cup of the mascarpone and 2 tablespoons of the mint, and taste for seasoning.

Ladle into wide, warm bowls or tall mugs, dollop on a little more mascarpone, and sprinkle with the remaining tablespoon mint. Serve immediately.

Soupe au Pistou

This is a fantastic, light and brothy soup that I just adore in spring. If you like a more substantial soup, however, reduce the amount of broth by one cup.

(recipe continues on page 134)

2 tablespoons extra-virgin olive oil

2 small yellow onions, finely chopped

3 carrots, quartered lengthwise and cut into ½-inch pieces

4 small zucchini, quartered lengthwise and cut into ¾-inch pieces

6 ounces green beans, ends trimmed, cut into 1-inch lengths

4 large white button mushrooms, brushed clean and quartered

3 garlic cloves, very finely chopped

1 cup canned diced Italian plum tomatoes, drained

1¾ quarts (7 cups) low-sodium chicken or vegetable broth, homemade (page 230 or 231) or store-bought

One 15-ounce can small white beans, rinsed and drained

2 tablespoons finely chopped fresh basil

½ teaspoon kosher salt

Freshly ground black pepper

Pistou (recipe below)

PISTOU

2 garlic cloves

1½ cups loosely packed fresh basil leaves

¾ cup loosely packed fresh flat-leaf parsley leaves

½ cup extra-virgin olive oil

¾ cup grated Parmesan cheese

Freshly ground black pepper

Place a large, heavy soup pot or Dutch oven over medium heat and add the oil. Add the onions and cook, stirring, until softened, about 5 minutes. Add the carrots, zucchini, and green beans and cook, stirring occasionally, until slightly softened, about 5 minutes. Add the mushrooms and garlic and cook, stirring, until the mushrooms give up their liquid, 1 to 2 minutes more.

Add the tomatoes and broth and increase the heat to medium-high. Bring to a boil, then reduce the heat to low and simmer, partially covered, until the vegetables are tender and the soup is slightly thickened, about 15 minutes.

Stir in the white beans, basil, salt, and pepper to taste and cook, uncovered, until warmed through and slightly thickened, about 10 minutes more.

To prepare the pistou: in a food processor, process the garlic until finely chopped. Add the basil and parsley, and pulse until finely chopped. Add the oil and pulse again, until chunky and evenly blended. Transfer to a small bowl and fold in the cheese and pepper.

Ladle soup into warm bowls and top with a large dollop of the pistou.

NOTE

Pistou is a French cousin to the Italian favorite, pesto, but contains no pine nuts. It was once considered "peasant food" all across the southwest region of France!

Thai Shrimp and Chicken Soup (Tom Kha Kai)

From the kitchen of Chantima Suka

SERVES 6 TO 8

Kaffir lime leaves are an integral part of Thai cooking, and every Thai family has a kaffir lime tree in their house or garden, according to Chantima—or, as we call her, Jim. Luckily, they are also available in Asian markets and some well-stocked supermarkets. The frozen leaves are easier to find, but they're not as pungent as the fresh leaves, so quantities should be doubled. If you can't find kaffir lime leaves at all, it's fine to make this soup without them—just increase the lemongrass to three stalks. Standard limes are sometimes used as a substitute, but Jim doesn't like the resulting flavor.

(recipe continues on page 137)

2 stalks lemongrass, pale yellow inner parts only, sliced

10 fresh kaffir lime leaves or 20 frozen leaves (see headnote on page 135)

¼ pound fresh galangal or ginger, peeled and thickly sliced

1 medium red onion, sliced thick

1½ quarts (6 cups) low-sodium chicken broth, homemade (page 230) or store-bought

One 15.5-ounce can unsweetened coconut milk

4 to 6 tablespoons tom yum paste (available at Asian and well-stocked markets)

2 tablespoons sugar

1 pound boneless skinless chicken breasts, cut into 1-inch pieces

One 15-ounce can baby corn, drained and halved crosswise

½ pound white button or cremini mushrooms, brushed clean and quartered

1 pound large shrimp, peeled and deveined

½ cup fresh lime juice, or more to taste

¼ cup Thai or Vietnamese fish sauce, or more to taste

Hot cooked rice or rice noodles, for serving

1 cup (about 4 ounces) snow peas, for garnish (optional)

½ cup roughly chopped fresh cilantro, for garnish

In a large, heavy soup pot or Dutch oven, combine the lemongrass, lime leaves, galangal, red onion, and broth. Cover the pot and bring to a boil, then reduce the heat to low and simmer gently for about 20 minutes.

Strain the broth through a fine meshed strainer and return the broth to the pot; discard the solids.

Return the broth to a low simmer and stir in the coconut milk, tom yum paste and sugar. Simmer gently, stirring occasionally, for about 2 minutes. Add the chicken and baby corn and cook for 10 minutes more.

Add the mushrooms and shrimp and cook until the shrimp are bright pink and cooked through, 5 to 6 minutes.

Remove from the heat and stir in the lime juice and fish sauce. Taste for seasoning. Ladle into large bowls over rice. Blanch snow peas, if using, in lightly salted boiling water for 1 minute, then rinse under cold running water. Sprinkle on top of each bowl. Scatter with the cilantro and serve.

Meatball Soup with Swiss Chard

SERVES 4 TO 6

Adding the chard at the end of the cooking time keeps it bright green and fresh, while the meatballs add a welcome and filling meaty component. Ideally, cook these tasty meatballs in a cast-iron skillet, to avoid sticking.

¼ cup plain dry breadcrumbs

½ pound ground pork

½ pound ground beef

⅓ cup very finely chopped onion

2 garlic cloves, very finely chopped

¼ cup golden raisins, finely chopped

2 tablespoons finely chopped fresh oregano or 2 teaspoons dried

½ teaspoon kosher salt

Freshly ground black pepper

1 tablespoon extra-virgin olive oil

1¾ quarts (7 cups) low-sodium chicken broth, homemade (page 230) or store-bought

1 bunch green Swiss chard, stems cut crosswise into ½-inch pieces and leaves cut crosswise into 1-inch strips

One 15-ounce can red kidney beans, rinsed and drained

1 teaspoon red pepper flakes

In a large bowl, combine the breadcrumbs, pork, beef, onion, garlic, raisins, oregano, salt, and plenty of black pepper. With a fork, combine until evenly mixed (do not overmix, or the meatballs will be tough). With clean hands, roll into 1-inch balls.

Place a large skillet over medium heat and add the oil. Cook the meatballs, in batches if necessary, until golden brown and cooked through, turning over occasionally, 8 to 10 minutes. Remove from the heat.

In a large, heavy soup pot or Dutch oven, bring the broth to a boil, then reduce the heat to medium-low. Add the meatballs, chard stems, beans, and pepper flakes; return to a simmer and cook until the meatballs are tender and juicy and the chard stems are almost tender, about 8 minutes.

Add the chard leaves and continue cooking just until wilted, about 4 minutes more. Taste for seasoning.

Ladle into warm bowls and serve immediately.

Frogmore Stew

This rustic, colorful, and soul-satisfying soup hails from the earliest days of South Carolina's island culinary tradition (it's sometimes called lowcountry boil). Simple to prepare, it takes very little time to satisfy and nourish both the meat- and seafood-lovers in your home. Add a few hunks of crusty bread, and—presto!—you've covered every possible food group for your family.

4 quarts (16 cups) cold water

2½ pounds small red potatoes, scrubbed

4 stalks celery, cut into 1-inch lengths

1 medium yellow onion, roughly chopped

½ cup Old Bay seasoning

1 garlic head, papery outer skin removed, halved crosswise

4 ears corn, shucked and each cut crosswise into 4 pieces

2 pounds smoked sausage, cut into 1½-inch lengths

1 pound crab legs (optional)

2 pounds medium-large shrimp, unpeeled (devein)

Kosher salt and freshly ground black pepper

Place a large, heavy soup pot or Dutch oven over medium-high heat and add the water, potatoes, celery, onion, Old Bay seasoning, and garlic and bring to a boil. Reduce the heat to medium and simmer until the potatoes are tender, 15 to 20 minutes.

Add the corn, sausage, and crab legs (if using) and continue cooking until the corn is tender, 3 to 4 minutes.

Add the shrimp and simmer until pink, 3 to 4 minutes more.

Taste for seasoning and add salt and pepper, if necessary. Discard the garlic pieces, if desired.

Ladle the stew into warm bowls, distributing all the chunky ingredients evenly, and serve immediately.

Summer Favorites

Catherine, Andrew, Sarah and Remick at the Cliffs of Moher in Ireland.

From the first week of June until the end of August, summer in Washington, D.C., is hot and humid. It is safe to say most activity takes place indoors on summer afternoons—the hottest part of the day. That's why here, in Summer Favorites, I've assembled lots of fabulous soups that are designed to be served chilled; they help to cool down your family while still providing everyone with a nice, nourishing meal.

June is also the time for graduations and Father's Day, plus family birthdays for Sarah and the twins, Catherine and Andrew. Last year, we attended three college graduations—in three different locations—for Sarah, Catherine, and Andrew.

Many of my summer soups feature luscious fresh tomatoes and tender sweet corn, simply because I adore their flavor. In summertime both are abundant at our local farmer's markets and colorful roadside produce stands.

Here, you will get to sample Chef Martin's Round Hill Gazpacho, which our family refers to as "chilled salad soup in a bowl." He tops his soup with grilled organic vegetables and herbs, and adds a splash of sweet balsamic vinegar to this tempting warm-weather soup. Also in this chapter is my own long-time summer favorite, Quick Gazpacho, a version for those days when you don't have time to cut perfectly dice your vegetables.

Chris, Andrew and Bo in the field.

Chef Martin with his team by the beautiful blue Caribbean Ocean at Round Hill, Montego Bay, Jamaica.

Since we can never get enough tomatoes in the summer, I continue the theme with three more classic tomato soups: Cold Tomato-Dill Soup, Old-Fashioned Tomato Soup with Maple-Candied Bacon, and finally Cream of Eggplant and Cherry Tomato Soup. Although tomatoes feature or star in all these savory, bright orange soups, they are very different. Be sure to try them all during the next tomato season!

Summer simply wouldn't be the same without mugs of hearty chowder. In July, I look forward to our vacation on Martha's Vineyard, where on chilly, rainy days I satisfy my hungry family with Vineyard Clam Chowder or Corn Chowder. Both are so simple to make, and take full advantage of the local summer bounty.

Luckily, the island is blessed with lots of good fish markets, offering fresh local fish and lobster, so this is when I like to prepare my Summer Bouillabaisse. The light broth, perfumed with fennel and rich seafood, makes this just one of the family's many Summer Favorites—I know you will enjoy them all!

right: The Wallace Seniors in Cumberland Island.

Quick Gazpacho

This popular summer soup has been a family tradition since I first started learning to cook. I began making this soup because of the vegetable garden the children and I planted each summer. From July until October, our garden produced so many juicy tomatoes, cucumbers, and delicious peppers that throwing together this tasty soup was a snap! I like to call this a nutritious, non-fat, cold salad in a bowl. Although it is not a traditional Spanish herb, I love the flavor of cilantro here, and it has become my own special garnish!

8 large ripe tomatoes, peeled and seeded (see Tip below)

4 large cucumbers, peeled and seeded (see Tip below)

2 large garlic cloves, pressed

2 cups V8 juice

2 cups low-sodium chicken broth, homemade (page 230) or store-bought

⅓ cup red wine vinegar

3 to 4 tablespoons extra-virgin olive oil

2 green or red bell peppers, cored and seeded

5 scallions, ends trimmed and finely chopped

1 bunch fresh cilantro, leaves only, chopped

¾ teaspoon kosher salt

6 drops Tabasco sauce, or to taste

Garlic croutons, for garnish (optional)

⅓ cup sour cream, for garnish (optional)

Roughly chop 4 of the tomatoes and 2 of the cucumbers. Set the remaining 4 tomatoes and 2 cucumbers aside.

In a food processor, combine the roughly chopped tomatoes and cucumbers with the garlic. Process until very smooth.

Transfer to a large bowl and stir in the V8, broth, vinegar, and oil.

Dice the remaining 4 tomatoes, 2 cucumbers, and the green bell peppers. Stir into the soup. Fold in the scallions, cilantro, salt, and Tabasco. Cover and refrigerate for at least 4 hours, or overnight.

Thirty minutes before serving, chill individual soup bowls, mugs, or stemless wineglasses. Ladle into bowls and, if desired, garnish with croutons and/or a dollop of sour cream.

TIPS

Peeling Tomatoes: **Bring a saucepan three-fourths full of water to a boil. Cut a very shallow cross in the smooth end of the tomatoes and drop them into the boiling water (if peeling more than 4 tomatoes, it's easier to do this in two batches). After 20 seconds, scoop up the tomatoes with a slotted spoon, transfer to a colander, and set under cool running water to stop them from cooking further. With a small, sharp knife, peel the skin.**
Seeding Cucumbers: **Halve the peeled cucumber lengthwise. Place the tip of a small spoon at the top of the seed channel, press in firmly, and scrape downward, scooping out the seeds.**

Round Hill Gazpacho

Chris and I like to sneak away alone after the Christmas holiday, when all our kids have returned to school or their own homes. Every year, we go to Round Hill resort in Montego Bay, Jamaica, for a vacation. It was there that I discovered Chef Martin's gazpacho, which is the ideal lunch by the blue Caribbean, refreshing and cool after a relaxing morning in the sun. The crunchy organic vegetables combined with the sweet balsamic vinegar really pop in your mouth! Nothing could be lighter or more delicious!

2 slices white bread, crusts removed

3 pounds ripe tomatoes, peeled and seeded

2 cucumbers, peeled and seeded

1 small red onion, coarsely chopped

2 green bell peppers, cored, seeded, and coarsely chopped

3 garlic cloves, minced or pressed

6 tablespoons extra-virgin olive oil

3 tablespoons red wine vinegar

Kosher salt

Balsamic vinegar

Croutons, for garnish

Soak the bread in a small bowl of water for 5 minutes. Drain and squeeze firmly to remove excess water.

As you prepare the vegetables, reserve about ⅓ cup each of the finely chopped tomato, cucumber, red onion, and pepper, for garnish. Refrigerate until ready to serve

Coarsely chop the remainder of the tomato, cucumber, red onion, and pepper, and add to blender or processor. Add garlic, oil, and red wine vinegar. Puree and transfer to a large bowl.

Cover the soup and the garnishes and refrigerate for at least 4 hours or overnight. Taste for seasoning and add salt and balsamic vinegar to taste.

Serve in chilled bowls, mugs, or wineglasses and garnish each serving with a pinch of finely chopped vegetables and 2 or 3 croutons.

Cold Tomato-Dill Soup

SERVES 8 TO 10

This cold soup is another summer dog day favorite in our household! We like to enjoy it when the tomatoes are ripe and when there is plenty of fresh dill available. Served with a grilled cheese panini featuring more fresh herbs (such as parsley or basil), it makes a light and refreshing lunch!

(recipe continues on page 151)

8 tablespoons (1 stick) butter

2 large yellow onions, roughly chopped (about 4 cups)

3 garlic cloves, very finely chopped

Feathery leaves from 1 large bunch fresh dill, roughly chopped, plus additional sprigs, for garnish

¾ teaspoon kosher salt

Freshly ground black pepper

2½ quarts (10 cups) low-sodium chicken or vegetable broth, homemade (page 230 or 231) or store-bought

Two (28-ounce) cans plus one 14.5-ounce can whole Italian plum tomatoes, drained and seeded

2 teaspoons ground allspice

¼ teaspoon sugar

Grated zest of 1 scrubbed lemon

1 cup yogurt, for garnish

In a large, heavy soup pot or Dutch oven, melt the butter over low heat. Add the onions and cook, covered and stirring occasionally, until tender and translucent, about 15 minutes. Add the garlic and cook, covered and stirring occasionally, for 2 minutes more.

Add half of the dill leaves, salt, and pepper to taste. Cook, uncovered and stirring frequently, for 15 minutes.

Add the broth, tomatoes, allspice, and sugar. Bring to a boil, then reduce the heat to low and simmer, covered, for 45 minutes. Add the lemon zest; remove from the heat and let cool for 5 to 10 minutes.

In batches, process the soup in a blender or food processor until smooth. (Hold the top of the blender firmly with a folded towel to prevent an explosion of hot soup.)

Return the soup to a clean pot or large bowl. Cool to room temperature. Meanwhile, finely chop the remaining dill leaves. Stir the chopped dill into the soup, cover tightly, and refrigerate overnight.

Just before serving, taste for seasoning. Ladle into chilled bowls and garnish each serving with a large dollop of yogurt and a sprig of dill.

Chilled Shrimp and Cucumber Soup

Here is another of our favorite chilled soups. This elegant soup requires almost no cooking, and is ready in minutes. The cool shrimp and cucumber combined with the fresh dill is both refreshing and filling on a hot summer day. I love to serve this soup in chilled glass bowls—beautiful!

2 large English cucumbers, peeled and coarsely chopped. (If the cucumber has any seeds, remove them.) (see Tip, page 147)

¼ cup white wine vinegar

2 teaspoons sugar

1 teaspoon kosher salt

1¼ pounds very small shrimp, peeled and deveined

2 tablespoons butter

¼ cup dry vermouth or white wine

Freshly ground black pepper

1½ cups buttermilk, very cold

½ cup plain yogurt

Feathery leaves from about ½ bunch fresh dill, or more to taste, plus additional sprigs, for garnish

In a large bowl, combine the cucumber, vinegar, sugar, and salt. Toss and let stand for 10 minutes.

In a colander, rinse the shrimp under cold running water. Drain well and transfer to a double thickness of paper towels.

In a small skillet, melt the butter over low heat. Add the shrimp, then increase the heat to medium-high and toss until the shrimp are pink, 2 to 3 minutes.

With a slotted spoon, transfer the shrimp to a small bowl; reserve the pan juices.

Add the vermouth to the skillet and boil until it is reduced to a few tablespoons; pour over the shrimp. Season very lightly with salt and pepper.

Drain the cucumbers in a colander and transfer to a food processor. Process briefly, then add the buttermilk and yogurt; continue to process until smooth. Add the dill leaves and process another few seconds, until the soup is a lovely pale green color.

Refrigerate the soup and the shrimp separately, covered, for at least 2 hours, or until very cold. Chill bowls or stemless wineglasses for serving.

Divide the shrimp evenly among the chilled bowls, and pour some soup over the top. Garnish with a sprig of dill and serve immediately.

Tomato–Sweet Corn Soup

SERVES 4 TO 6

Sweet, summer white corn is abundant all along the East Coast, and it's long been a big favorite with our vegetable-loving family. It was a natural for me to create a soup that takes advantage of this wonderful, seasonal treat.

TIPS

- *Cold mixtures require more assertive seasoning with salt and pepper; be sure to taste just before serving, and adjust to your family's taste.*
- *Summer is corn time all across the country, but if for any reason fresh corn is unavailable, by all means use thawed frozen corn.*
- *To remove corn from the cob, stand a well-shucked cob on end in a large bowl and shave downward with a large, heavy knife. Adjust the angle of the knife as necessary so that you remove the whole kernel, but not too much of the tough base.*

1½ tablespoons extra-virgin olive oil

1 small white onion, finely chopped

5 or 6 large ripe tomatoes (about 3 pounds), cored, seeded, and coarsely chopped (see Tip, page 154)

2 tablespoons all-purpose flour

1½ tablespoons tomato paste

3 cups white corn kernels (from about 6 ears of corn; reserve the corncobs and cut them in half crosswise)

20 large leaves fresh basil, divided

½ teaspoon kosher salt

Freshly ground black pepper

1 quart (4 cups) low-sodium chicken or vegetable broth, homemade (page 230 or 231) or store-bought

½ cup best-quality store-bought mayonnaise

1 teaspoon grated zest from a scrubbed and dried lemon

Place a large, heavy soup pot or Dutch oven over medium heat and add the oil. Add the onion and cook, stirring occasionally, until slightly softened, about 4 minutes. Add the tomatoes and cook, stirring occasionally, until slightly softened, about 3 minutes more.

Stir in the flour and cook, stirring constantly, for 2 minutes more. Stir in the tomato paste, corn kernels, corncobs, 15 of the basil leaves, salt, pepper to taste, and broth. Bring to a boil, then reduce the heat to low and simmer gently for 30 minutes. Remove from the heat and discard the corncobs. Let cool for 5 to 10 minutes.

In batches, process the soup in a food processor until very smooth. (Hold the top of the blender firmly with a folded towel to prevent an explosion of hot soup.)

Strain the soup through a fine-mesh sieve or cheesecloth into a large bowl, pressing down hard on the solids. Discard the solids. Cool to room temperature, then cover and refrigerate for at least 4 hours or overnight, until thoroughly chilled.

Chill bowls for serving and finely chop the remaining 5 leaves of basil. In a small bowl, whisk together the chopped basil, mayonnaise, and lemon zest. Taste the soup for seasoning and adjust with salt and pepper.

Ladle the soup into chilled bowls and garnish with a dollop of the lemon-basil mayo. Serve immediately.

Corn Chowder

SERVES 6

This corn chowder is sweet and creamy in taste and texture. It's a family favorite in the late summer, when corn is abundant throughout the area.

156

3 tablespoons extra-virgin olive oil, divided

6 slices thick-cut smoked bacon

1 yellow onion, finely diced

3 russet potatoes, peeled and cut into 1-inch cubes

¼ teaspoon red pepper flakes

1 quart (4 cups) half-and-half

3 cups whole milk

3 cups corn kernels (from about 6 ears of corn)

½ teaspoon kosher salt

Freshly ground black pepper

¼ teaspoon cayenne pepper

In a large skillet, warm 1 tablespoon of the oil. Add the bacon and cook until golden brown and crisp. Transfer to paper towels to cool, then crumble and reserve.

Place a large, heavy soup pot or Dutch oven over medium-low heat and add the remaining 2 tablespoons of the oil. Add the onion and cook, stirring occasionally, until translucent, about 5 minutes. Add the potatoes and pepper flakes, and cook 2 minutes more, to just glaze the vegetables.

Add the half-and-half and milk and bring up just to a simmer (watch carefully—dairy products can boil over in an instant!). Reduce the heat to low and simmer gently until the potatoes are tender, about 10 minutes. Add the corn, salt, and black pepper to taste and cook for 5 minutes more. Stir in the cayenne.

Using a slotted spoon, transfer about 4 cups of the vegetables to another pot.

Cool the remaining soup mixture for 5 minutes. In batches, process in a blender or food processor until smooth. (Hold the top of the blender firmly with a folded towel to prevent an explosion of hot soup.)

Pour the blended soup mixture over the remaining vegetables in the original pot, and warm through. Taste for seasoning, and adjust with salt and black pepper.

Ladle into wide mugs, scatter with the crumbled bacon, and serve immediately.

Yellow Squash Soup

Whenever we travel in the summer, leaving our vegetable garden to its own devices, we return home to find large yellow squash, zucchini, and cucumbers. Our black Labrador, Bo, would proudly bring these huge vegetables to our back door. The young children claimed they were grown for the Big Friendly Giant (BFG), a classic Roald Dahl story about a giant who refused to eat humans and so lived on sour vegetables called "snozzcumbers."

Summer squash does grow rapidly in the garden (especially in late summer); this soup is a quick and simple remedy to take advantage of the giant vegetable issue. This bright soup can be frozen for up to three months. Defrost, reheat, and be sure to adjust the seasoning before serving.

3 tablespoons extra-virgin olive oil

1 medium yellow onion, finely chopped

6 medium yellow summer squash (or 2 to 3 larger squash), ends trimmed and finely sliced

2 garlic cloves, very finely chopped

½ teaspoon kosher salt

Ground white pepper

1 quart (4 cups) low-sodium chicken broth, homemade (page 230) or store-bought

1 cup buttermilk, very cold

4 tablespoons finely chopped fresh flat-leaf parsley

2 tablespoons finely snipped fresh chives

1 tablespoon fresh lemon juice

NOTE

Although it will be a different color, this soup is equally delicious and appealing made with pale green pattypan squash, or any other summer squash available at your local farmer's market or from your own vegetable garden.

Place a large, heavy soup pot or Dutch oven over medium-low heat and add the oil. Add the onion and cook, stirring occasionally, until slightly softened, about 3 minutes. Add the squash, increase the heat to medium, and cook, stirring occasionally, until the squash just begins to brown, about 5 minutes. Add the garlic, salt, and pepper to taste and cook for 1 minute more.

Add the broth and bring to a boil. Reduce the heat to low and simmer gently, covered, until the squash is tender, about 15 minutes. Remove from the heat and cool for 5 to 10 minutes.

In batches, process the soup in a blender or food processor until smooth. (Hold the top of the blender firmly with a folded towel to prevent an explosion of hot soup.)

Transfer the soup to a serving bowl and cool to room temperature. Cover and refrigerate until chilled, 5 to 6 hours (or overnight). Chill individual bowls or glasses for serving.

Just before serving, stir in the buttermilk, 2 tablespoons of the parsley, the chives, and lemon juice. Taste for seasoning and adjust with salt and pepper as necessary.

Ladle into chilled soup bowls, and garnish with a pinch of the remaining parsley.

Vineyard Clam Chowder

SERVES 10 TO 12

Larsen's Seafood Market is located in Menemsha, on the island of Martha's Vineyard.

Betsy Larsen—who owns this wonderful market—gave me this recipe. Last summer, I learned an important lesson when I decided to make this soup for the family on a rainy day. Well, it looked beautiful, but I'm afraid it tasted like a sand bar. (I'd thought I would be clever, and used the water that I soaked the clams in for the broth. Big mistake! Be sure to soak and rinse the clams thoroughly, and do not use the leftover liquid!) On the Vineyard and throughout the Cape Cod area, strained frozen clam juice is usually available from the local fishmongers.

(recipe continues on page 162)

Vichyssoise with Watercress Salad Soup

SERVES 8

For Father's Day, Chris loves to have a barbecue and enjoy a relaxing family afternoon with the children. Our daughter Megan is a vegetarian, so while everyone else is wolfing down beef and pork, I always make sure she enjoys a nice meal: I make plenty of grilled vegetables, which I sprinkle with hard goat cheese.

And because Father's Day falls on Sunday, of course we also need soup! We often start with this creamy French classic, which is perfect for a warm June afternoon and satisfies the meat-eaters as well. But we enjoy this soup for lunch all summer long—with the watercress salad piled on top, we get our soup and salad in one!

TIPS
- I always prepare the vichyssoise the day before, then let it chill overnight. This ahead-of-time preparation lets me enjoy quality time with our children, and the flavor of the soup definitely improves!
- Remember that cold mixtures require more aggressive seasoning with salt and pepper than hot mixtures. Taste before seasoning and adjust to your family's taste.
- For a more elegant and special occasion, I like to serve this pale soup in delicate white wine glasses. In this case, omit the watercress salad topping (in other words, you will only need 1 bunch of watercress, and quantity of lemon juice and olive oil will be reduced). Then, after ladling the soup carefully into the glasses, garnish each one with a pinch each of chopped chives and lemon zest.

(recipe continues on page 165)

3 tablespoons extra-virgin olive oil, divided

4 leeks, white and light green parts only, well washed and coarsely chopped

2 pounds red or white potatoes, peeled and coarsely chopped

2 bunches watercress, (tender stems and leaves only), divided

2¼ quarts (9 cups) low-sodium chicken or vegetable broth, homemade (page 230 or 231) or store-bought

¾ teaspoon kosher salt

Ground white pepper

1 cup half-and-half

1½ tablespoons fresh lemon juice, divided

Grated zest of 1 scrubbed lemon

2 tablespoons finely snipped fresh chives

Place a large, heavy soup pot or Dutch oven over medium heat and add 2 tablespoons of the oil. Add the leeks and cook, stirring frequently, until tender, about 5 minutes (do not allow to brown). Add the potatoes and cook, stirring occasionally, until slightly softened, about 5 minutes more.

Add half of the watercress and cook, stirring, just until wilted, about 3 minutes more. Add the broth, salt, and pepper to taste. Bring to a boil, then reduce the heat to low and simmer gently, partially covered, until the vegetables are very tender, about 25 minutes. Remove the soup from the heat and let cool for 5 to 10 minutes.

In batches, process the soup in a blender or food processor until very smooth. (Hold the top of the blender firmly with a folded towel to prevent an explosion of hot soup.)

Transfer the soup to a large bowl. Stir in the half-and-half and ½ tablespoon of the lemon juice. Cool to room temperature, then cover and refrigerate for at least 5 hours (or overnight). Refrigerate the remaining bunch of watercress separately.

Chill wide, shallow bowls. Taste the soup for seasoning and adjust with salt, pepper, and lemon juice as necessary.

Just before serving, toss the remaining watercress with the remaining tablespoon of lemon juice and remaining tablespoon of olive oil. Season to taste with salt and pepper.

Ladle into the chilled bowls and place a mound of the watercress salad on top. Scatter with a pinch each of lemon zest and chives, and serve immediately.

Summer Bouillabaisse

SERVES 8 TO 10

*I love the way this simple Summer Bouillabaisse looks with the
shrimp tails left on. Instead of cooked lobster, you can also use
raw lobster tail meat; if so, add it along with the cod and shrimp.
If the feathery green fronds are still attached to the fennel,
roughly chop about ⅓ cup and scatter on the finished soup as
a final garnish.*

- 2 tablespoons extra-virgin olive oil
- 2 large bulbs fennel, quartered, cored, and thinly sliced crosswise
- 4 stalks celery, thinly sliced
- 4 garlic cloves, thinly sliced
- 2½ cups dry white wine
- 1 bay leaf
- Two 28-ounce cans Italian plum tomatoes, seeded, with juice
- 2 pounds cod, halibut, or monkfish, skin and bones removed and cut into 2-inch chunks
- 1½ pounds large shrimp, peeled (tails left on) and deveined
- 2 teaspoons red wine vinegar
- ½ teaspoon kosher salt
- Freshly ground black pepper
- 1 pound cooked lobster meat, cut into large chunks (optional)
- 1 cup mayonnaise
- 2 teaspoons fresh lemon juice
- 1¼ teaspoons smoked or regular paprika
- 1½ tablespoons finely chopped fresh tarragon

Place a very large, heavy pot over medium-high heat and add the oil. Add the fennel and celery and toss to coat well with the oil. Cook, stirring occasionally, until softened and slightly golden, about 5 minutes. Add the garlic and cook, stirring, for 1 minute more.

Add the wine and bay leaf and bring to a simmer. Roughly chop the tomatoes and add with their juice; partially cover the pot and cook until the tomatoes begin to break down, 6 to 8 minutes.

Add the cod and shrimp and cook, covered, until all the seafood is firm, 6 to 9 minutes, stirring once halfway through. Stir in the vinegar, salt, and pepper to taste. Add the lobster, if using, and warm through for 2 minutes. Taste for seasoning. Discard bay leaf.

Meanwhile, whisk together the mayonnaise, lemon juice, and paprika in a small bowl.

Ladle the soup into warm bowls, distributing all the ingredients evenly. Top with a dollop of paprika mayo and a pinch of tarragon.

TIP

Feel free to substitute any firm-fleshed white fish (preferably from a sustainable species), such as halibut, monkfish, or flounder, for the cod.

Old-Fashioned Tomato Soup with Maple-Candied Bacon

SERVES 4

This is one of the first soups I remember from my childhood. When I had to stay at home, feeling slightly feverish, my mom served this simple soup with a creamy grilled cheese sandwich; it always made me feel much better. There may be nothing in the world that beats tomato soup and melted cheese. Adding the decadent, sweet-smoky bacon elevates the soup to gourmet heaven.

(recipe continues on page 170)

8 slices thick-cut applewood-smoked bacon

2 tablespoons maple sugar or light brown sugar

1 tablespoon butter

1 tablespoon extra-virgin olive oil

1 small yellow onion, finely chopped

1 sprig fresh rosemary

1 bay leaf

4 garlic cloves, sliced

2 tablespoons tomato paste

One 28-ounce can Italian plum tomatoes, drained and seeded

1½ teaspoons kosher salt

Freshly ground black pepper

½ teaspoon granulated sugar

1¼ cups low-sodium chicken broth, homemade (page 230) or store-bought

¼ cup heavy cream

Preheat the oven to 400°F. Line a rimmed baking sheet with parchment paper. Arrange the bacon on the parchment and bake for 8 to 12 minutes (depending on thickness), turning over once, until crisp. With bunched-up paper towels, blot the fat from the baking sheet and sprinkle bacon with the maple sugar. Bake for 6 minutes more, until glazed. Set aside.

Place a medium, heavy soup pot or Dutch oven over medium heat and add the butter and oil. When the butter has melted, add the onion, rosemary, and bay leaf. Cook, stirring frequently, until the onion is softened, about 5 minutes. Add the garlic and cook, stirring, for 1 minute, then reduce the heat to medium-low and add the tomato paste. Cook, stirring for a minute or two to cook off the raw taste of the tomato paste, then add the tomatoes and cook, stirring occasionally, until the tomatoes begin to break down, about 6 minutes. Add the salt, a pinch of pepper, the granulated sugar, and the broth. Stir to mix and bring to a boil.

Reduce the heat to low and simmer gently, partially covered, for 10 minutes. Stir in the cream and remove from the heat. Let cool, uncovered, for 5 minutes.

Discard the rosemary sprig and bay leaf and transfer to a blender or food processor. Process until very smooth. (Hold the top of the blender firmly with a folded towel to prevent an explosion of hot soup.) Return to the saucepan and warm through over medium heat.

Ladle into wide, warm bowls, and serve with 2 pieces of bacon perched on the edge of each bowl.

Cream of Eggplant and Cherry Tomato Soup

SERVES 6

This is a bright orange soup that is easy to prepare for your family in the summer, when eggplants and cherry tomatoes are abundant at farmer's markets. The addition of eggplant gives this soup depth and texture. If you have an herb garden, it is a joy to harvest your own luscious summer basil, which adds lightness and tang to this delicious soup.

1 medium eggplant (about 1 pound), peeled and sliced about ¾ inch thick

Extra-virgin olive oil, for brushing

1 medium onion, roughly chopped (about 1½ cups)

1 stalk celery, roughly chopped

2 pounds whole cherry tomatoes

3 whole garlic cloves, peeled

3 cups low-sodium chicken broth, homemade (page 230) or store-bought

¾ cup heavy cream

2 tablespoons grated Parmesan cheese

½ teaspoon kosher salt

Freshly ground black pepper

18 whole fresh basil leaves, torn into pieces, for garnish

Preheat the oven to 400°F. Brush both sides of the eggplant slices with a little oil. In a large roasting pan, arrange the eggplant slices in a single layer. Roast for 20 minutes, until golden and slightly softened. Scatter the onion, celery, tomatoes, and garlic over the eggplant and roast for 25 minutes more, until all the vegetables are softened and beginning to brown.

Transfer half of the vegetables to a food processor and puree with half of the broth. Transfer to a large, heavy soup pot or Dutch oven and repeat with the remaining vegetables and broth.

Place the pan over medium heat and stir in the cream, cheese, salt, and pepper to taste. Bring just to the simmering point, stirring occasionally, and taste for seasoning.

Ladle into warm bowls and scatter with the basil.

Friends
and Family
Favorites

The Dubin family in their garden. Harry, Robin, Liz, Dick, and Louis. Photo by Hadar Goren Photography.

In this chapter, I want to share some of the fantastic soups I have gathered from our travels, friends, and memorable family experiences. I find it very exciting to recreate these warm and wonderful soups from, and for, my family and friends.

Over the years as I created new and tasty soups, I also collected them—from friends, in-laws, famous restaurants, and great chefs, all of whom I pestered after sampling their specialties. From the legendary '21' Club, to Washington's classic institution, the Jockey Club, to the wonderful Hillwood Museum, no one could escape from my recipe requests!

My dear friend Elizabeth Dubin makes a delectable Maryland Crab Soup, the recipe for which has been in her family for decades. It takes two days to make, in a 10-gallon soup pot with 15 pounds of meat and vegetables! I like to make Liz's soup in August, when crabs are plentiful, then freeze it to enjoy when crabs are no longer in season.

Crab feasts are a beloved summertime tradition throughout the Virginia and Maryland bay area and shore retreats. At a crab feast you sit at a big table covered with brown paper, and buckets of steaming-hot, spicy crabs are piled high in front of you. Everyone uses their fingers to pry out the juicy morsels of crab, and washes it all down with plenty of cold beer. In this chapter, you will find our friend Adam's Day-After-Crab-Feast Soup, which is delicious and simple to prepare—as long as you have extra crabs on hand. (Since the crabs are so delicious, the only way to ensure enough leftovers for this soup is to order double the amount you and your family could conceivably consume!)

Chris's parents: Mike and Mary Wallace.

Chris's sister Pauline with her husband, Richard. Photo by Peter Simon.

Master butcher Pamela Ginsberg of Wagshal's Market not only assists me in selecting the best-quality meats, locally grown vegetables, and fish in town, she also kindly shared her very famous recipe for New Orleans–style gumbo. This is one you'll want to set aside a weekend to prepare—and you'll never forget it!

Even my weekly yoga group has been tapped to contribute their favorite soups. Three of my wonderful friends—Tracy, Mariella, and Arline—have contributed recipes from their travels and family traditions. Recently, we started a soup club, and once a month one of us brings a pot of soup to warm up and share after our workouts.

Last, but certainly not least, my wonderful family and their favorite soups are big players in this chapter. From Nana's No-Cream Broccoli Soup to my sister-in-law Pauline's Minestrone, plus our son Peter's Engagement Cheese Soup—you'll enjoy the soups and the stories that go with them. Finally, the tale of our extraordinary evening with Mike and Mary at Rao's restaurant in Harlem may bring a tear to your eye—just the way it did to ours!

right: Nana at home in Jupiter, Florida, with Catherine and Andrew.
opposite: Jennifer and Peter on their wedding day. Photo by Craig Paulsen.

FRIENDS AND FAMILY FAVORITES

'21' Club Chilled Senegalese Soup

SERVES 10

I first learned about Senegalese soup in my twenties when, on very special occasions, I went to the '21' Club in New York City with my mother. It's one of the few places in which this traditional soup is still served. In the Wallace family, twenty-first birthdays are always celebrated at the '21' Club. When Catherine and Sarah turned twenty-one, Chris carried on the tradition, flying up to New York just to be sure "Dad" could take his girls to this legendary club on their big birthdays.

On a hot summer day, I like to serve my Senegalese soup (inspired by the one we enjoyed at the '21' Club) cold in my ceramic cabbage bowls on the side garden terrace. It's a wonderful start to an outdoor evening supper.

1 quart (8 cups) water

1 tablespoon extra-virgin
   olive oil

1½ teaspoons kosher salt,
   divided

2 boneless skinless chicken
   breasts (about 7 ounces
   each)

2 tablespoons butter

3 Granny Smith apples, peeled,
   cored, and diced

2 large carrots, peeled and
   finely chopped

1 large white onion, finely
   chopped

¼ cup raisins

1 garlic clove, minced

3 tablespoons curry powder

2 tablespoons all-purpose flour

2 quarts (8 cups) low-sodium
   chicken broth, homemade
   (page 230) or store-bought

½ cup heavy cream

Freshly ground black pepper

Mango chutney, from a jar,
   for garnish

NOTE

Chicken breasts can be dry and tough if overcooked. Here, I allow the residual heat of the poaching water to gently cook the chicken after the pan is removed from the heat. This technique yields tender, juicy chicken

Place a large skillet with a snug-fitting lid over medium-high heat and add the water, oil, ½ teaspoon of the salt, and the chicken breasts. Bring to a simmer, then immediately remove the pan from the heat. Cover and let stand until tender, about 12 minutes.

Lift the chicken breasts from the broth and let cool on a plate. Cut into large dice. Cover and refrigerate until 10 minutes before you plan to serve the soup.

In a large, heavy soup pot or Dutch oven, melt the butter over medium heat. Add the apples, carrots, onion, raisins, and garlic. Cook, stirring occasionally, until softened, about 10 minutes.

Stir in the curry powder and cook for 1 minute, then add the flour and stir constantly for 2 minutes, until blended into a paste and sizzling. Add the broth and bring to a boil. Reduce the heat to low, cover, and simmer gently for about 1 hour and 15 minutes (check occasionally to be sure the broth is not boiling furiously; reduce the heat further as necessary).

Stir in the cream, the remaining 1 teaspoon salt, and pepper to taste. Remove from the heat and let cool for 5 to 10 minutes.

In batches, process the soup in a blender or food processor until very smooth. (Hold the top of the blender firmly with a folded towel to prevent an explosion of hot soup.) Transfer to a large bowl, cover, and refrigerate until well chilled and the flavors have had time to marry, about 3 hours (or overnight).

Remove the soup and chicken from the refrigerator and let stand for 10 minutes. Ladle the soup into wide, shallow bowls and garnish with a jumble of chicken dice and a teaspoon of mango chutney.

Jockey Club Senegalese Soup

SERVES 8 TO 10

The Jockey Club is located not far from our home in Washington, at the Fairfax Hotel. It looms large in my memories of growing up. I celebrated my twenty-first birthday, my mother's fiftieth birthday, and my engagement lunch at the Jockey Club. I always like to order this warm version of Senegalese soup. The soup is thickened with potatoes instead of the flour used in the '21' Club version, and the chicken is folded into a tasty mayonnaise-based salad. It's a wonderful concoction, fragrant with Indian spices, that the waiter slowly pours into your bowl, over tender chicken salad, right at the table. Any home cook can replicate this historic soup in their own kitchen, just as I have.

2 skinless, boneless chicken breast halves (about 1 pound)

2 teaspoons extra-virgin olive oil

Kosher salt and freshly ground black pepper

2 tablespoons butter

1 large white onion, finely chopped

3 small Granny Smith apples, peeled, cored, and sliced

1 russet potato, peeled, quartered lengthwise, and sliced

1 tablespoon plus 1 teaspoon curry powder, divided

1¼ teaspoons ground turmeric, divided

2 quarts (8 cups) low-sodium chicken broth, homemade (page 230) or store-bought

⅓ cup heavy cream

2 teaspoons fresh lemon juice

½ cup best-quality store-bought mayonnaise

¼ cup golden raisins, finely chopped

3 tablespoons finely chopped fresh flat-leaf parsley

Preheat the broiler to high heat. Brush both sides of the chicken breasts with the oil and season with salt and pepper. Broil for about 6 minutes on each side, until golden brown and cooked through to the center. Let cool, cut into small dice, cover and refrigerate.

In a large, heavy soup pot or Dutch oven, melt the butter over medium-low heat. Add the onion, apples, and potato and cook gently, stirring occasionally, until softened, about 15 minutes. Stir in 1 tablespoon of the curry powder and 1 teaspoon of the turmeric, and cook for 1 minute more. Add the broth, ¾ teaspoon salt, and pepper to taste. Bring to a boil, then reduce the heat, partially cover the pot, and simmer until all the vegetables are very tender, 25 to 30 minutes.

Let stand for at least 5 minutes. In batches, puree the soup in a blender or food processor. (Hold the top of the blender firmly with a folded towel to prevent an explosion of hot soup.) Transfer to a large bowl, cool to room temperature, then refrigerate to allow the flavors to marry, at least 3 hours (or up to overnight).

To serve: Transfer the soup to a large, clean saucepan. Place over medium heat and when the soup comes to a simmer, stir in the cream and lemon juice, and remove from the heat. Taste for seasoning; adjust with salt, pepper, and/or lemon juice as desired.

In a medium bowl, whisk together the mayonnaise, the remaining 1 teaspoon curry powder, the remaining ¼ teaspoon turmeric, the raisins, and salt and pepper to taste. Fold in the diced chicken.

Place a spoonful of the chicken-mayonnaise salad in the base of each wide, shallow bowl. Ladle the warm soup over the top, scatter with a little parsley, and serve.

Pam's New Orleans Gumbo

From the kitchen of Pamela Ginsberg

SERVES A CROWD

Wagshal's Market, in Spring Valley, is one of my favorite food shops in Washington. Pamela Ginsberg is the master butcher who oversees the market, and she always helps me in selecting the best meats, locally grown vegetables, and fish in town. Pam has worked for several prominent New Orleans chefs and is famous for her gumbo. Local schools and charities often request that she donate a pot of this delicious concoction as an auction item. For authentic gumbo flavor and color, you will make a roux that is the color of chocolate—just like in New Orleans. Pamela has simplified this recipe so it can be made fairly easily, and trust me, it is worth the effort!

TIPS

• *Pamela often makes the stock and the vegetable-shrimp base for the gumbo the night before. Then, she stirs it into the roux and finishes the gumbo on the day of serving.*

• *Throughout the South, the roux is considered a crucial part of the cooking culture. Everyone has their own technique, but it's easy as long as you stir constantly, and never let the mixture get so hot that it turns black.*

• *You will need two large pots (ideally, 10-quart capacity). In one, you will make the stock, and later the shrimp. In the other you will make the gumbo itself. (If one pot is larger than the other, reserve the largest pot for the gumbo.)*

• *Be careful not to add too much roux, which would result in a too-thick gumbo— you can always add more but you cannot take it back. Also, use salt sparingly.*

(recipe continues on page 182)

FOR THE STOCK

4 kosher chicken legs with thighs attached, rinsed and patted dry

1 stalk celery with leaves, coarsely chopped

1 whole, peeled onion

4 garlic cloves, finely chopped

12 soup crabs, halved and cleaned

One 5-pound bag fully cooked and seasoned crawfish

Leftover shrimp heads, tails, and shells (from the vegetable-shrimp mixture below)

¼ cup kosher salt

2 tablespoons freshly ground black pepper

FOR THE VEGETABLE-SHRIMP MIXTURE

2 large yellow onions, coarsely chopped

2 large red bell peppers, cored, seeded, and coarsely chopped

2 large yellow bell peppers, cored, seeded, and coarsely chopped

1 large green bell pepper, cored, seeded, and coarsely chopped

2 stalks celery, coarsely chopped

Two 28-ounce cans Italian plum tomatoes, drained, and coarsely chopped (reserve juice)

½ cup Worcestershire sauce

To make the stock: In a large stockpot, combine the chicken legs, celery, onion, garlic, crabs, 4½ pounds of the crawfish, shrimp heads, tails, and shells, salt, and pepper and cover with cold water. Bring to a boil, then reduce the heat and simmer partially covered for 2 to 2½ hours.

Remove the chicken legs and let them cool. Discard the fat and bones from the legs and shred the meat and set aside. When the stock has cooled almost to room temperature, strain it through a large colander lined with cheesecloth to remove all the seafood and herbs, rendering a semi-clear broth. Discard the crabs and crawfish. Do not rinse the stockpot—you will use it again to cook the shrimp.

To make the vegetable-shrimp mixture: In a very large pot (a "gumbo pot," 10 quarts or larger), combine the onions, peppers, celery, tomatoes, Worcestershire sauce, ¼ cup of the vinegar, garlic, thyme, 2 tablespoons of the Creole seasoning, Tabasco, and cayenne to taste. Add the reserved shredded chicken meat.

Stir the strained stock into the vegetable-chicken mixture.

In the now empty stockpot, combine the shrimp, the remaining 3 tablespoons Creole seasoning, and the remaining ¼ cup vinegar. Place over high heat, cover, and cook the shrimp until they turn slightly pink, 4 minutes.

Transfer the shrimp and all their juices to the vegetables in the gumbo pot, and add the okra, if desired.

½ cup white vinegar, divided

12 garlic cloves, chopped

¼ cup fresh thyme leaves, coarsely chopped

5 tablespoons Creole seasoning, divided

¼ cup Tabasco sauce, or to taste

Cayenne pepper

3 pounds large shrimp, peeled and deveined (reserve heads, tails, and shells for stock above)

Two 10-ounce bags frozen okra, thawed (optional)

FOR THE GUMBO

8 tablespoons (1 stick) butter

⅓ cup all-purpose flour

2 pounds large cooked shrimp, peeled and deveined

2 pounds crawfish tail meat with fat

1 pound colossal crabmeat

1 pound Andouille sausage, halved lengthwise, and cut into half-moons

Hot cooked white rice, for serving

2 scallions, light and dark green parts only, trimmed and coarsely chopped

1 bunch fresh curly parsley, coarsely chopped

Bring the mixture to a boil, then reduce the heat to low and simmer gently for 1½ hours. (If desired, make this mixture the night before; cool to room temperature and refrigerate, covered. Return to a simmer before finishing the gumbo as below.)

To make the gumbo: First, make the roux: in a large cast-iron skillet, melt the butter. Gradually add the flour, whisking all the time to make a thin, smooth paste. Whisking constantly and vigorously, cook the mixture over medium-low heat for 45 minutes to 1 hour, until it reaches a milk chocolate–like color.

Add the roux to the simmering gumbo pot mixture a little at a time, stirring frequently, until it reaches the desired thickness; you may not need to add all the roux.

Add the cooked shrimp, crawfish tail meat, crabmeat, and sausage. Continue cooking just until warmed through; do not allow to boil, or the seafood may become tough.

Serve immediately over white rice, topped with the scallions and parsley, and garnished with the remaining whole crawfish.

Tracy's Hearty Vegetable Salad Soup

SERVES 8

This recipe comes from Tracy Hackett, who is my friend and our family health guru. If you want to pour off and discard half the bacon fat before cooking the vegetables, go ahead and do so.

TIPS

- *If half your family eats their soup at noon, and the other half isn't ready for lunch, just keep the spinach chilled, and it will stay fresh and crisp until serving time.*
- *Dried mushrooms must be reconstituted in very hot water before using. The soaking water is full of flavor and can be used to intensify the flavor of your soup. If desired, you could also use fresh shiitake mushrooms here. (Use 4 ounces stemmed fresh shiitake mushrooms, and increase the chicken broth by 1 cup, to make up for the lack of mushroom-soaking liquid.)*

- ½ cup of dried morel or shiitake mushrooms (about 1 ounce)
- 6 slices thick-sliced, center-cut bacon, cut into thick strips
- 1 small onion, finely chopped
- ½ pound scrubbed fingerling or new potatoes, roughly chopped
- 3 large carrots, peeled, halved lengthwise, and sliced ¼ inch thick
- 3 stalks celery, sliced ¼ inch thick
- 2 garlic cloves, minced or pressed
- 1 cup thawed frozen white corn or kernels from 2 ears fresh corn
- ¼ cup roughly chopped canned artichoke hearts
- 1 jarred roasted red pepper, roughly chopped
- One 14.5-ounce can cannellini beans, rinsed and drained
- 2 quarts (8 cups) low-sodium chicken broth, homemade (page 230) or store-bought
- ½ teaspoon dried oregano
- ¼ teaspoon chili powder
- ¼ teaspoon ground cumin
- ¼ teaspoon smoked or regular paprika
- ¼ teaspoon ancho chile powder
- ½ teaspoon kosher salt
- 8 ounces baby spinach leaves (about 8 cups)
- Green Tabasco sauce, for serving

Soak the morel mushrooms in 1½ cups boiling water for 30 minutes. Drain, reserving the soaking liquid; roughly chop the mushrooms.

In a large, heavy soup pot or Dutch oven, cook the bacon over medium-low heat until golden and crisp. With a slotted spoon, transfer to paper towels.

To the same pot, add the onion, potatoes, carrots, and celery and cook, stirring frequently, until the vegetables are slightly browned, about 5 minutes. Add the garlic and cook, stirring, for 1 minute more.

Stir in the cooked bacon, soaked mushrooms, corn, artichoke hearts, red pepper, and beans. Add the mushroom-soaking liquid, broth, oregano, chili powder, cumin, paprika, ancho chile powder, and salt. Bring to a boil, then reduce the heat to low and simmer gently, partially covered, for 45 minutes. Taste and adjust for seasoning.

Ladle the hot soup into 8 wide shallow bowls. Top with a handful of spinach and serve immediately. Pass a bottle of green Tabasco sauce at the table.

Family Wellness Soup

SERVES 8

Chantima Suka is from Thailand, and she has been helping our family for over six years now. We call her Jim, and when she first began working for us, our daughter Sarah came down with mononucleosis near the end of her senior year of high school! Jim concocted this super-simple soup of chicken and vegetables, and it has become our family tradition for treating colds and most other ailments.

This soup is a natural cure-all, and works wonders for getting your loved ones on the road to recovery.

1 tablespoon butter

1 large onion, finely chopped

8 boneless skinless chicken thighs (about 2 pounds), cut into 1-inch cubes

6 stalks celery, finely chopped

8 carrots, peeled and coarsely chopped

2 quarts (8 cups) low-sodium chicken broth, homemade (page 230) or store-bought

1 teaspoon dried thyme

1 teaspoon dried oregano

1 teaspoon kosher salt

Freshly ground black pepper

In a large, heavy soup pot or Dutch oven, melt the butter over medium-low heat. Add the onion and cook, stirring occasionally, until tender, about 5 minutes.

Increase the heat to medium and add the chicken to the pot. Cook for about 10 minutes, turning over two or three times, until golden brown and firm.

Add the celery, carrots, broth, thyme, oregano, salt, and pepper to taste.

Increase the heat and bring to a boil, then reduce the heat to low, cover, and cook at a gentle simmer until the vegetables are tender, about 1 hour.

Taste for seasoning and serve.

Arline's Carrot-Ginger Soup

SERVES 6 TO 8

My yoga friend, Arline, came over for Thanksgiving dinner one year, and brought her favorite soup. This brightly colored and flavored soup carries a big punch of ginger. She originally got the recipe in Belgium from an Alaskan friend's French husband's Bulgarian chef. What an international delicacy! Serve hot or cold, any time of year.

2 tablespoons butter

2 medium onions, finely chopped

1½ pounds sweet young carrots, peeled and thinly sliced

3 tablespoons finely chopped peeled fresh ginger

1½ quarts (6 cups) low-sodium chicken or vegetable broth, homemade (page 230 or 231) or store-bought

1 cup whole milk

1½ cups half-and-half

1 teaspoon kosher salt

1 teaspoon ground white pepper

In a large, heavy soup pot or Dutch oven, melt the butter over medium-low heat. Add the onions and cook, stirring occasionally, until very soft, about 15 minutes. Add the carrots and ginger and continue cooking for 20 minutes more, stirring occasionally.

Add the broth and bring to a boil, then reduce the heat to low and simmer gently, partially covered, for 20 minutes. Remove from the heat and let stand for 10 minutes, uncovered.

In batches, puree in a blender or food processor. (Hold the top of the blender firmly with a folded towel to prevent an explosion of hot soup.)

Return to a clean pot and stir in the milk, half-and-half, salt, and pepper. Warm through over low heat and taste for seasoning before serving.

Cuban Black Bean Soup

From the kitchen of Mariella Mayor Gonzalez

SERVES 6 TO 8

The luscious smell that will fill your home when you make this soup is one that is very familiar to Cuban families. This is my friend Mariella's mother's recipe, and it has been in her family since they lived in Havana in the 1920s. It is her husband and son's favorite dish, and when she kindly shared it with us, it became one of our favorites, too. You can serve this soup alone, or on top of white rice with a side of plantains. When you are ready to serve the soup, don't forget to make yourself a nice mojito!

(recipe continues on page 190)

1 pound dried black beans, rinsed and picked over

3 tablespoons extra-virgin olive oil

1 yellow onion, finely chopped

1 green bell pepper, cored, seeded, and finely chopped

5 garlic cloves, chopped

1½ quarts (6 cups) water

¼ cup dry sherry

2 tablespoons kosher salt

1 teaspoon freshly ground black pepper

1 tablespoon sugar

2 teaspoons dried oregano

2 bay leaves

Hot cooked white rice and fried plantains, for serving (optional)

In a very large bowl, soak the beans overnight in water to cover by at least 2 inches (they will expand a lot). Drain well.

Place a large, heavy soup pot or Dutch oven over medium-low heat and add the oil. Add the onion and bell pepper and cook slowly, stirring occasionally, until the vegetables are very tender and slightly golden (this is called a *sofrito*), 8 to 10 minutes. Add the garlic and cook, stirring, for 1 minute more.

Add the drained beans, water, sherry, salt, black pepper, sugar, oregano, and bay leaves. Bring to a boil, then reduce the heat to low and simmer, partially covered, for 1 hour and 45 minutes. (If you like a thicker soup, simmer uncovered.)

When the beans are very tender, discard the bay leaves and serve. If desired, ladle over rice and serve fried plantains on the side.

Nana's No-Cream Broccoli Soup

From the kitchen of Vana Martin

SERVES 6

"Nana" is what we have all called my mother since my children were born. During the winter, our family spent vacations in Jupiter, Florida, at Nana's home, where we enjoyed many festive meals right on the beach.

I used to wonder why my mom would serve a hot soup in a hot climate. Well, now I understand this British tradition, because of our annual trips to Jamaica (a former British colony). Hot soup is on the menu every day at Round Hill, our new winter vacation destination. My mom still lives in Jupiter, and I love to visit her and try her latest soup recipes. This is the one that our family requested most often.

Here, tons of vegetables and mashed potatoes thicken the broth, making it seem like a cream-based soup.

(recipe continues on page 193)

2 tablespoons butter, divided

1 medium yellow onion, finely chopped

1 stalk celery, finely chopped

2 leeks, white and light green parts only, well washed and thinly sliced

1 bay leaf

6 cups broccoli (small florets and peeled, sliced stalks)

1½ quarts (6 cups) low-sodium chicken broth, plus additional broth if needed

3 russet potatoes, peeled and cut into 1-inch cubes

1 cup half-and-half

1½ teaspoons kosher salt

Freshly ground black pepper

Place a large saucepan over medium-low heat and add 1 tablespoon of the butter. When it has melted, add the onion, celery, leeks, and bay leaf. Cook, stirring occasionally, until the vegetables are tender, about 10 minutes.

Add the broccoli and broth and bring to a boil, then reduce the heat to low and simmer gently, partially covered, for about 25 minutes, until the vegetables are tender. Remove from the heat and discard the bay leaf. Let cool while you cook the potatoes.

In a large pot, cover the potatoes with water, bring to a boil, and cook until tender, about 45 minutes. Drain well and return to the empty pot. Add the remaining 1 tablespoon butter, the half-and-half, salt, and pepper to taste. With a potato masher, mash until smooth.

In batches, puree the soup in a blender or food processor, until smooth. Transfer the puree to the pot with the mashed potatoes. (If the soup is too thick, thin with a little more broth, a tablespoon at a time.)

Reheat the soup over medium-low heat and taste for seasoning; adjust with salt and pepper. Serve in warm bowls.

NOTE
Garnish each bowl of soup with a reserved broccoli floret, or store-bought croutons, if desired.

Maryland Crab Soup

From the kitchen of Liz Dubin

Memorial Day each year we join our dear friends Elizabeth and Richard Dubin for a Monday afternoon lunch at their beautiful home in Bethesda, Maryland, to wrap up the first long weekend of summer.

Liz always includes this delicious soup in her scrumptious buffet; it has been in her family for decades. We love having seconds and even thirds of this rich lump crabmeat soup. I finally persuaded her to give me the recipe last year, and she delivered the soup and the written recipe to our door as a holiday present. It takes her two days to make, in a 10-gallon pot with 15 pounds of meat and vegetables!

Spice-steamed Maryland blue crabs are beloved in the D.C. area and a true treat to savor throughout the summer. Note that the spice rub is very flavorful, so be careful when adding salt to this soup. In fact, you may not need any at all.

FOR THE STOCK

1½ pounds thick-sliced bacon, cut into strips

2 large white onions, roughly chopped

1 whole head of garlic, roughly chopped

1 bunch celery, very roughly chopped

1 pound carrots, peeled and cut into chunks

2½ pounds beef stew meat

Kosher salt and freshly ground black pepper

2 tablespoons canola oil

4 smoked ham hocks

10 beef short ribs

FOR THE CRAB SOUP

2 cups cooked pearl barley

Six 28-ounce cans tomato sauce

Three 2-pound bags frozen mixed vegetables , thawed

1 dozen spice-steamed blue crab claws, legs, and bodies, cleaned (see Tip below)

5 pounds back-fin crabmeat

⅓ cup Old Bay seasoning, or to taste

10 tablespoons chili powder, or to taste

¼ cup Tabasco sauce, or to taste

3 pounds additional colossal or jumbo lump crabmeat, for garnish

To make the stock: In a large pot (preferably 10-gallon) brown the bacon over medium-low heat. Add the onions and garlic and cook, stirring, until softened, about 8 minutes. Add the celery and carrots and cook, stirring.

Meanwhile, season the stew meat with salt and pepper. In a large skillet, heat the oil over medium-high heat. Brown the meat until golden, turning over with tongs. Add to the pot along with the ham hocks and short ribs.

Cover with water and bring to a boil. Reduce the heat to low, partially cover, and simmer gently for 4 hours.

Discard all the bones, vegetables, and fat; cut the meat into pieces and reserve. Strain the stock through a colander lined with cheesecloth, and return the stock to the cleaned pot.

To make the crab soup: To the stock, add the reserved meat, barley, tomato sauce, mixed vegetables, crab claws, legs, and bodies, back-fin crabmeat, Old Bay seasoning, chili powder, and Tabasco. Add a little more water to keep the ingredients barely covered, if necessary. Partially cover the pot, bring to a boil, then reduce the heat to low and simmer for 1 to 1½ hours.

Serve in wide, warm bowls. Spoon a generous amount of colossal crabmeat on top of each.

TIP
To clean steamed, spicy Maryland crabs: remove the outer shell and cut the crab in half. Pull away the "devils" (also known as "dead man's fingers," or gills) and any intestinal matter.

Adam's Day-After-Crab-Feast Soup

SERVES 6 TO 8

I originally met Adam Mahr through one of my oldest friends, Ronald; Ronald and I shared an apartment in D.C. when I was twenty. Now, Adam has become a dear friend of our family, too. He owns one of the most beautiful housewares shops in Georgetown, called A Mano. When he is not traveling around the world, he entertains beautifully. This is his special Day-After-Crab-Feast Soup. It is simple and delicious. All you have to do is make sure you have enough crabs left over to make it—always order double what you think you will eat!

1½ tablespoons canola oil

1 pound beef chuck steak or roast, cut into ¾-inch cubes

6 garlic cloves, minced

2 quarts (8 cups) water

1 cup beer

One 28-ounce can peeled tomatoes, drained

One 28-ounce can tomato sauce

Two 10-ounce bags frozen mixed vegetables (thawed)

1 yellow onion, chopped

1 cup chopped green cabbage

1 russet potato, peeled and cut into ½-inch chunks

6 whole spice-steamed blue crabs, halved and "devil" removed

1 pound large shrimp, peeled and deveined

1 pound crabmeat (preferably back-fin or the best available)

2 tablespoons distilled white vinegar

Old Bay seasoning

Freshly ground black pepper

Tabasco sauce

Place a large, heavy soup pot or Dutch oven over medium-high heat and add the oil. Add the beef and sear until golden on all sides, about 8 minutes. Tip the pan and spoon off as much fat as possible. Reduce the heat to low, add the garlic and cook, stirring, until golden, 1 to 2 minutes.

Add the water and beer and bring to a boil. Reduce the heat to medium-high and add the tomatoes, tomato sauce, mixed vegetables, onion, cabbage, and potato. Add the crabs and continue cooking for 30 minutes.

Add shrimp and crabmeat and cook until the shrimp is pink, 3 to 4 minutes.

Add the vinegar, Old Bay seasoning, pepper, and Tabasco sauce to taste. Serve in warm bowls.

TIPS
- *Old Bay seasoning is very flavorful, so be careful when adding salt to this soup. You may not need any at all.*
- *Adam says: "While it's my favorite dish for the day after a crab feast, you can also steam fresh blue crabs to make this soup. In your crab pot, combine 1 part water, 1 part beer, 1 part white cider vinegar, ½ cup sea salt, ½ cup Old Bay seasoning, and 6 whole garlic cloves—then steam until done. Of course, if you are near the ocean, add one cup seawater!"*

Engagement Cheese Soup

This recipe comes from the Old Drover's Inn, a former Relais & Châteaux property outside New York City that has since closed. My son and daughter-in-law introduced me to it, so it holds a very sentimental place in our family.

Jennifer and Peter's courtship began a decade ago, when my father-in-law, Mike Wallace, introduced them. The day before their visit to the inn, Jennifer had been in Bosnia on a story for 60 Minutes. When she got back, Peter whisked her away to upstate New York for a romantic dinner. Peter pretended to just stumble upon the inn. When they arrived, Jennifer was in jeans. But Peter had packed a surprise bag complete with clothes and shoes so she could dine at the restaurant in style. Their first course was the Cheddar cheese soup, a perfect, hearty soup to take the chill off a cool night. After a delicious meal, they retired to the library, where Peter got down on one knee and proposed.

Jennifer has been a truly wonderful addition to the Wallace family. We've loved her and this recipe ever since!

(recipe continues on page 200)

8 tablespoons (1 stick) butter

1 small yellow onion, finely chopped

1 small green bell pepper, cored, seeded, and finely chopped

1 carrot, peeled and finely chopped

1 stalk celery, finely chopped

½ teaspoon kosher salt

Freshly ground black pepper

½ cup all-purpose flour

½ teaspoon dry mustard

1¼ quarts (5 cups) low-sodium chicken or vegetable broth, homemade (page 230 or 231) or store-bought

2 tablespoons medium-dry or Amontillado sherry

4 cups shredded sharp Cheddar cheese (about 12 ounces)

1 teaspoon Worcestershire sauce

In a large, heavy soup pot or Dutch oven, melt the butter over medium-low heat. Add the onion, bell pepper, carrot, and celery and cook, stirring occasionally, until softened, about 6 minutes.

Add the salt and black pepper to taste. Stir in the flour and mustard to make a paste, and cook, stirring frequently, to cook off the raw taste of the flour, about 3 minutes more.

Stir in the broth and sherry until smooth; increase the heat and bring to a simmer. Reduce the heat to medium-low and cook, stirring frequently, until slightly thickened, about 4 minutes.

Add the cheese and stir constantly until melted and smooth, just 1 to 2 minutes. Do not let it boil!

Stir in the Worcestershire sauce and taste and adjust the seasoning. Ladle into warm bowls.

> TIP
> *If you like, make the popovers on page 35, excluding the blue cheese. Serve the popovers warm, on the side.*

Hillwood Museum Borscht

SERVES 6

Nestled on twenty-five acres in the middle of Rock Creek Park is a jewel of an estate, museum, and gardens formerly owned by Marjorie Merriweather Post, the American collector and heiress to the Post cereal empire. You are minutes from downtown, but feel as if you are off in the countryside.

It holds many fond memories for me because it is one of the first places Chris took me to celebrate my birthday in April to enjoy a wondrous spring afternoon. Seeing the Fabergé egg collection, Russian and Sèvres porcelains and strolling the many different gardens made Hillwood a favorite of mine to visit.

Now, each season I enjoy visiting Hillwood with my lady friends for a cultural afternoon. We make reservations at the café to enjoy a luscious lunch that begins with a bowl of their borscht. The experience takes you back to another era.

(recipe continues on page 203)

8 ounces (½ pound) applewood-smoked bacon, cut into small dice

1 large carrot, cut into medium dice

2 small red bell peppers, cored, seeded, and cut into medium dice

1 white onion, cut into medium dice

2 quarts low-sodium beef broth, homemade (page 232) or store-bought

8 ounces (½ pound) red beets, peeled and cut into small dice

8 ounces (½ pound) beef stew meat, cut into small dice

2 tablespoons granulated garlic

2 to 3 dried bay leaves

8 ounces (½ pound) Yukon gold potato, peeled and cut into medium dice

¼ of a small head white cabbage, shredded (about ½ cups, loosely packed)

Kosher salt and freshly ground black pepper

GARNISHES

Sour cream

Chopped fresh dill

Toasted rounds of bread

In a large, heavy soup pot or Dutch oven, cook the bacon until crisp and golden. Add the carrot, pepper, and onion and cook gently over low heat, stirring occasionally, until just tender, 10 to 12 minutes.

Add the beef broth, beets, stew meat, granulated garlic, and bay leaves and bring to a boil. Reduce the heat and simmer gently for 15 to 20 minutes (the beets should still be firm at this point).

Add the potato and simmer until both the beets and potatoes are tender, 10 to 15 minutes more. Add the cabbage and remove the pot from the heat. Cover and let stand until the cabbage is tender, 5 to 7 minutes. Remove the bay leaves.

Season to taste with salt and pepper. Ladle into warm bowls and top with a dollop of sour cream. Scatter with the dill and serve with a slice of toasted bread on the side.

Italian Wedding Soup

Published with the permission of Frank Pellegrino

SERVES 6

Every summer Chris and I vacation on Martha's Vineyard, where we spend cherished time with Chris's parents, Mary and Mike Wallace. We have met and made friends with many wonderful people during these magical times. One of the special couples we have become close to is Nancy Ellison and Bill Rollnick. She is a top photographer and he is an enormously successful businessman. But the point of this story is that they introduced us to Rao's—perhaps the toughest restaurant reservation to get in New York City.

Located on 114th Street in East Harlem, it looks like the quintessential Italian "joint"—with a bright red entrance down a few steps from the sidewalk, as well as year-round Christmas decorations. The food is truly fabulous, and it is known— justifiably or not—for a clientele straight out of The Sopranos. In fact, co-owner Frank Pellegrino portrayed FBI agent Frank Cubitoso on the popular show.

But what makes Rao's feel truly special is that it's impossible to get into. There are only ten tables, and every night, each table is, in effect, "owned" by a long-time customer. On their particular night, each customer either eats at "their" table, or lends the table to a friend. And you can be sure no table at Rao's ever goes empty. Outsiders need not apply. (The restaurant doesn't answer the phone, and if they did, it would still be impossible to get a reservation.)

Chris had been talking for years about how much he wanted to go to Rao's. When he found out Nancy and Bill have a booth there every Monday night, we arranged to borrow their table months in advance. When the appointed date arrived, we took Mary and Mike along to share in our evening of feasting on delicious home-style Italian dishes. Late in the evening, Frank Pellegrino turned on the jukebox and began to sing along to classic songs from the 50s and 60s. As it turned out, this was the week Mike announced he was finally retiring from 60 Minutes, after 40 incredible years on the show. Frank declared he would dedicate a song to Mike, and he sang Sinatra's "My Way"—changing the words to "He did it HIS way." There was not a dry eye in the house, especially not at our table.

One of the memorable dishes we had that night was Rao's Wedding Soup. Frank says he grew up eating it in East Harlem. And when I asked him to share his recipe, he sent it to all of you with his love. Buon appetito!

(recipe continues on page 206)

- 1 head escarole, washed and cored
- 1 head chicory, washed and cored
- 1 head Savoy cabbage, cleaned, cored, and cut into eighths
- Two 19-ounce cans cannellini beans, undrained
- ¼ cup olive oil
- 4 to 5 garlic cloves
- ¼ pound pancetta, chopped
- ½ pound hot or sweet Italian sausage, casings removed
- One 28-ounce can imported Italian plum tomatoes, drained and hand-crushed
- Kosher salt and freshly ground black pepper to taste
- Pinch dried oregano
- ¼ pound dried hot or sweet sausage, peeled and chopped
- Freshly grated Parmigiano Reggiano cheese

Bring a large pot of generously salted water to a boil. Add the escarole, return to a boil, and cook until wilted, about 1 minute. Remove the escarole with a slotted spoon and set it aside. Boil the chicory in the same pot of water until wilted, about 1 minute, and remove it with a slotted spoon. Boil the cabbage in the same pot until wilted, about 2 minutes, and remove. Reserve 5 cups of the cooking water.

Meanwhile, in a food processor, puree 1 can of the cannellini beans with the juices. Set aside.

Heat the olive oil in a large pot over medium-low heat. Add the garlic and cook, stirring, until golden brown, about 2 minutes. Remove the garlic with a slotted spoon and discard.

Add the pancetta to the pot with the oil and cook, stirring, for 1 minute. Add the sausage meat and cook, stirring and breaking it up, until fully cooked through, 5 to 6 minutes. Add the pureed cannellini beans, bring to a rapid simmer, and add the crushed tomatoes. Season with salt, pepper, and oregano.

Raise the heat and bring to a boil. Add the cooked vegetables, the can of whole beans with their juice, the dried sausage, and the reserved water and return to a boil. Reduce the heat to low and let simmer for 30 minutes.

Taste and adjust seasoning. Serve with grated cheese.

Pauline's Minestrone

From the kitchen of Pauline Bourgeois

SERVES 6 TO 8 AS A MAIN COURSE

This is my sister-in-law Pauline's favorite soup! We always have a wonderful time when we go to New Canaan to visit her family. They have two yellow Labradors that our beloved dog, Winston, loves to visit, too. Both Pauline and her husband, Richard, are excellent cooks and always entertain us with scrumptious meals.

Serve this hearty soup the way Pauline does, with great bread, then follow with a pie, like apple or pumpkin. She often doubles this recipe, so the family has plenty of minestrone for dinner during the week.

½ cup extra-virgin olive oil

1 large yellow onion, thinly sliced

1 carrot, peeled and diced

1 stalk celery, diced

1 small russet potato, peeled and diced

1 medium zucchini, diced

1 cup diced green beans (about 4 ounces)

3 cups Savoy cabbage, thickly sliced

1½ quarts (6 cups) low-sodium beef broth, homemade (page 230) or store-bought

1 cup canned Italian plum tomatoes, with juice

Rind from a piece of Parmesan cheese (see Tip below)

½ teaspoon kosher salt

Freshly ground black pepper

One 14.5-ounce can cannellini beans, rinsed and drained

⅓ cup grated Parmesan cheese

Place a large, heavy soup pot or Dutch oven over medium heat and add the oil. Add the onion and cook, stirring frequently, until golden brown and softened, about 6 minutes.

Add the carrot, and cook, stirring occasionally, for 5 minutes. Then add the celery and cook, stirring occasionally to stop the vegetables from scorching, for about 5 minutes more.

Add, one at a time, cooking for a bit after each addition, the potatoes, zucchini, and green beans. All the vegetables should be nicely glazed and softened.

Add the cabbage and cook, stirring, for 10 minutes longer.

Stir in the broth, tomatoes and their juice, Parmesan rind, salt, and pepper to taste.

Reduce the heat to low, cover, and simmer gently, stirring occasionally, for 3 minutes.

If the soup is too thin and watery, continue simmering, uncovered, to thicken slightly. Or, if the soup is too thick, add a bit more broth.

Fifteen minutes before serving time, stir in the beans and taste for seasoning. Discard the Parmesan rind and ladle into warm bowls. Pass the grated cheese at the table.

> **TIP**
> *Never throw away the rind of a wedge of Parmesan cheese! As you use up a piece of cheese, save the rind in a baggie in the freezer. Add to almost any soup, to provide a little extra rich and tangy flavor.*

Game Day Favorites

above and opposite: Our big, burly ball player, Remick at work on the mound. Photo by Michael Babich.

When I met Chris and his children, I didn't know much

about team sports. I grew up playing tennis and competing in horse shows. Well, that changed quickly when we started attending pro football, basketball, hockey, and baseball games with our young and very active family. We even let the younger boys miss school on opening day for the Orioles baseball season (it was around then that I learned who Cal Ripken was, as I watched him break the record for consecutive games played). He has long since retired from baseball, and Washington now has its own young team, the Nationals, whose games we like to attend.

On Remick's sixth birthday, Andrew gave him his first baseball glove. When Andrew tried to throw him a baseball, it hit him in the face and Remick ran away, crying. Now, Remick pitches for the Rhodes College varsity baseball team. What a thrill it is to go to Memphis several times in the spring and cheer for his team, The Lynx, and watch our big, burley youngest son play ball. As you may be able to tell, I am just a little bit proud of him!

The Wallace family has been, and will always be a sports-oriented gang, and over the years I've created a collection of soups that fill up my favorite sports fans while we all sit together to watch and cheer for our teams on television.

There are four different types of chili in this chapter: Touchdown, "Buffalo," Ground Turkey and Black Bean Chili, and White Chili. Different cuts of meat, plus variations on herbs and spices make them very different from one another. As far as my hungry family is concerned, you can never have too many kinds of chili in your recipe box!

All-American Cheeseburger Soup is a simple, one-dish meal

that tastes just like its title would lead you to believe. Just add a toasted bun and crisp dill pickle, kick back, and let the games begin! And here's another fun soup with that similar, comfort-food style: my Baked Potato Soup is rich and creamy—and when topped with bacon, cheese, and chives, it is fully loaded and ready to satisfy your family for any sports night.

Chris and I are friends with several of the Washington team owners and attend many professional sporting events. But sometimes all of us would rather just stay at home, turn on the television, and enjoy one of my Game Day Favorites.

top: Remick with his new jersey from his brother Andrew.
above: Winston with his hamburger on game days!
right: Cal Ripken, Jr., with Andrew looking on in awe.

212

Touchdown Chili

SERVES 12

This is my "two kinds of beef" chili that I love to serve on big game days. I like to prepare this chili the day before a sporting event, so the flavors have time to marry, and the spice really kicks in.

When I was the baseball mom for Remick's high school team, I took this tasty chili in a slow cooker to the field on a blustery March day to feed the grateful players and their parents. I served it in individual Frito chip packets and let each person top their chili with chopped onion and cheese. I called the dish Frito pie, and it was a hit with everyone!

> **TIPS**
> • When browning meat, it is important not to crowd the pan, otherwise, the meat will steam instead of sear, and the flavor won't achieve its potential, rich beefiness.
> • Ask your butcher to grind the chuck on the larger disk of his grinder. Some butchers offer this as a chili mixture.

(recipe continues on page 215)

1 tablespoon canola or
    vegetable oil

2 cups finely chopped red bell
    peppers

1 cup finely chopped onion

½ cup finely chopped carrot

2 large garlic cloves,
    very finely chopped

1½ pounds ground light-meat
    turkey

1 tablespoon tomato paste

4 teaspoons chili powder

2 teaspoons ground cumin

½ teaspoon kosher salt

3 cups low-sodium chicken
    broth, homemade (page 230)
    or store-bought

One 5.5-ounce can V8 juice

Two 14.5-ounce cans black
    beans, rinsed and drained

Freshly ground black pepper

GARNISHES (OPTIONAL)

¼ to ½ cup finely diced white
    onion, to taste

1¼ cups shredded Cheddar
    cheese

⅔ cup sour cream

Place a large, heavy soup pot or Dutch oven over medium-low heat and add the oil. Add the bell peppers, onion, carrot, and garlic and cook, stirring frequently, until the vegetables are tender, about 12 minutes.

Increase the heat to medium-high and add the turkey. Cook, stirring and breaking up the meat, until the turkey is no longer pink, about 5 minutes. Stir in the tomato paste, chili powder, cumin, and salt and cook for 1 minute more.

Add the broth, V8 juice, and beans and bring to a boil. Reduce the heat and simmer gently, partially covered and stirring occasionally, until the chili thickens, about 1 hour. Taste for seasoning and adjust with salt and black pepper as necessary.

Ladle the chili into warm bowls and, if desired, garnish with onion, cheese, and sour cream.

White Chili

This is a fun variation on the chili theme because it is white in color and has a somewhat soupy consistency. When I started working with cookbook author Brigit Binns, I asked her to share her favorite white bean chili. She did, and our family loves my version of her classic dish. It has been a true delight for me to have such an extraordinary foodie to share ideas and recipes with for this cookbook. Not to mention, Brigit has a great sense of humor and is a beautiful friend. The garnishes of sour cream, scallions, and chopped cilantro make for a delicious, light meal for any game day. (The boys in my household wouldn't hear of chili without Cheddar cheese, so I've made it optional here!)

TIPS

• If fresh jalapeño chiles are unavailable, substitute well-drained canned green chiles from the Latino section of your supermarket.

• Dried beans are notoriously variable in their cooking time. Older beans, left on the shelf for a long time, will take far longer than fresher dried beans. If you purchase your dried beans from a reputable shop with brisk turnover, you are more likely to find the beans done after 1½ hours. The only solution is to check them frequently, starting after about an hour!

(recipe continues on page 222)

1 pound dried white beans, soaked in water to cover overnight

1½ quarts (6 cups) low-sodium chicken broth, homemade (page 230) or store-bought

1 whole jalapeño chile, seeded and finely chopped

3 bay leaves

1 tablespoon vegetable oil

2 pounds ground light-meat turkey

1 large onion, finely chopped

¾ teaspoon kosher salt

⅛ teaspoon cayenne pepper

5 garlic cloves, very finely chopped

2 tablespoons chili powder

1 tablespoon ground cumin

GARNISHES

½ cup sour cream

2 cups grated mild Cheddar cheese (optional)

8 scallions, white and light green parts only, finely chopped

¼ cup roughly chopped fresh cilantro

Drain the beans and pick over and discard any discolored beans or debris.

In a large, heavy soup pot or Dutch oven, combine the soaked beans, broth, jalapeño, and bay leaves (the broth should cover the beans by about 1½ inches; add a little water if necessary). Bring to a boil, then reduce the heat to very low, partially cover and simmer gently until the beans are tender, 1½ to 2¼ hours. Discard the bay leaves

Transfer 1 cup of the beans to a blender or food processor (add a little of the cooking liquid, so the mixture will move). Process until smooth, then stir the pureed beans back into the whole beans and set aside.

Place a large, heavy skillet over medium heat and add the oil. Add the turkey and cook, stirring and breaking up the meat, until no longer pink, about 10 minutes. Add the onion, salt, and cayenne and cook, stirring occasionally, until the onion is very soft and slightly golden, about 10 minutes. Add the garlic, chili powder, and cumin and cook, stirring, until the aromas are released, about 2 minutes. Stir this mixture into the beans and place the pot over medium heat. Bring up very slowly to a simmer, stirring occasionally. Cook until slightly thickened, about 15 minutes. Adjust the seasoning with salt and cayenne as necessary.

Ladle the chili into large, shallow bowls. Top with a dollop of sour cream and scatter with cheese (if using), scallions, and cilantro. Serve immediately.

Baked Potato Soup

This soup is just what the title says: a baked potato in a soup! It is rich and creamy and, when topped with the bacon, chives, and cheddar cheese—it is fully loaded and ready to please all of your gamers.

(recipe continues on page 225)

5 medium russet potatoes, scrubbed

3½ tablespoons butter, divided

3 cups whole milk

½ cup half-and-half

1¼ teaspoons fennel seeds

1 cup shredded Cheddar cheese, divided

¾ cup sour cream

1 teaspoon kosher salt

½ teaspoon ground white pepper

½ teaspoon celery salt

1½ cups low-sodium chicken broth, homemade (page 230) or store-bought

4 scallions, white parts only, finely chopped

5 slices bacon, cooked and diced

1 teaspoon finely snipped fresh chives

Preheat the oven to 350°F. Pat the potatoes dry and rub them all over with 1 tablespoon of the butter. Place on a baking sheet lined with aluminum foil and bake for about 1½ hours, or until tender. Remove from the oven and cool slightly.

In a small saucepan, combine the milk, half-and-half, and fennel seeds. Bring up to just below the boiling point (do not let it boil); immediately remove from the heat, and let the mixture cool slightly.

When the potatoes are cool enough to handle, cut them into quarters, and scoop the flesh of 3 of the potatoes into a food processor (reserve the last 2 potatoes, which you will add to the soup just before serving). To the food processor, add ½ cup of the cheese, the sour cream, salt, pepper, and celery salt.

Pour the milk mixture through a fine-mesh sieve, to remove the fennel seeds, into the food processor with the potatoes. Pulse the mixture until smooth.

Transfer the mixture to a large, heavy soup pot or Dutch oven and add the broth, scallions, remaining 2½ tablespoons butter, and the reserved cut-up potatoes. Place the pot over low heat and warm through, stirring frequently, for about 15 minutes.

Ladle into wide, warm bowls and garnish with the remaining ½ cup cheese, the bacon, and chives.

All-American Cheeseburger Soup

SERVES 6

This is the game day favorite of our younger sons Andrew and Remick; Chris was doubtful. But everything from your favorite cheeseburger is here in this satisfying one-pot dish. For the full cheeseburger experience, serve this dish with toasted sesame buns and kosher dill pickles. I especially like dipping the bun with the crisp dill pickle into this cheesy soup.

1 tablespoon extra-virgin olive oil

2 pounds lean ground beef

1 medium onion, chopped

2 stalks celery, diced

2 carrots, shredded

2 tablespoons finely chopped fresh basil

2 teaspoons finely chopped fresh flat-leaf parsley

2 garlic cloves, very finely chopped

2 tablespoons all-purpose flour

1½ quarts (6 cups) low-sodium chicken or beef broth, homemade (page 230 or 232) or store-bought

2 medium potatoes, peeled and cut into ½-inch chunks

One 14.5-ounce can diced tomatoes, drained

One 6-ounce can tomato paste

4 cups shredded Cheddar cheese

4 cups shredded Monterey Jack cheese

¼ cup ketchup

2 tablespoons Dijon mustard

1 cup whole milk

FOR SERVING

Toasted sesame hamburger buns

Kosher dill pickle slices

Place a large, heavy soup pot or Dutch oven over medium-high heat and add the oil. Add the beef, onion, celery, carrots, basil, parsley, and garlic and cook, stirring frequently to break up the meat, until the meat is browned and vegetables are tender, 6 to 8 minutes.

Remove from the heat briefly, and tip the pan to one side. Spoon off the accumulated fat from the mixture and return the pot to medium heat.

Sprinkle the flour over the beef mixture and cook, stirring all the time, for about 2 minutes to cook off the raw taste of the flour.

Stir in the broth and potatoes and bring to a boil, stirring occasionally. Reduce the heat to low and simmer gently, covered, until the potatoes are tender, about 10 minutes.

Stir in the tomatoes, tomato paste, cheeses, ketchup, and mustard. Cook, stirring all the time, until the cheeses are melted and smooth and the soup is only just coming to a gentle boil. Stir in the milk, and continue cooking just until heated through.

Ladle into wide, shallow bowls and serve with toasted buns and pickle slices on the side.

Stocks: Strong Families Start with Good Bones

I know that soups made from homemade broth taste better, and it's certainly a more economical choice if you have the time. When Chris is out of town, I often make a big batch of chicken, vegetable, or beef broth, then freeze it in 2- or 4-cup quantities, ready to pull it out on a Sunday morning when the colorful vegetables, fresh herbs, healthy dried beans and lentils, and other delicious flavorings are all ready for me to quickly create a nourishing soup for the family.

But you shouldn't feel guilty if you can't make your own broth—I certainly don't! Much of the time, I choose a high-quality boxed or canned chicken, vegetable, or beef broth, preferably organic, and always low in sodium. (Salt is an important part of the cooking process, but I prefer to add it myself rather than have it added in the packaging process: that way, I stay in control of what my family is eating, and I always want them to eat the best! And I'll always advise you to taste your soup just before serving, in case it needs more salt.)

Peter and Jennifer's wedding family photo in Gramercy Park in New York City: Andrew, Sarah, Lorraine, Peter, Jennifer, Chris, Catherine, Megah, and Remick. Photo by Craig Paulsen.

above: Andrew, Chris and Remick at a World Series game.
below: Me with Sarah and Remick in Martha's Vineyard.

This chapter includes a selection of homemade broths, but there's a third option: If you have just a little extra time, you can enrich and freshen a good store-bought broth by simmering it for 30 minutes to 1 hour with a little chopped onion, carrot, and celery (plus, if you have it, a chicken wing, drumstick, or back—perhaps you have some left over in your freezer). Strain everything out and use as directed.

Chicken Broth

6 pounds chicken bones (backbones, wings, but no fat)

2 large yellow onions, peeled and quartered

4 large carrots, washed and roughly chopped

6 stalks celery, roughly chopped

6 sprigs fresh thyme

1 bay leaf

7 quarts water

In a very large stockpot, combine the chicken bones, onions, carrots, celery, thyme, and bay leaf. Add the water and place the pot over high heat. Bring to a boil, then adjust the heat so the liquid simmers gently, and cook for 1 hour. As soon as the chicken begins to release fat into the liquid, after about 10 minutes, begin degreasing with a large flat spoon; degrease every 10 or 15 minutes. Skim the surface of any visible fat; don't worry if you can't remove every bit.

Strain through a fine-mesh sieve into a large, clean saucepan. Place over medium-high heat and simmer briskly until reduced by about half of its volume, to about 3½ quarts; this will take about 20 minutes. Continue degreasing the stock as it reduces, if necessary. Use the stock immediately as directed in the recipe, or cool to room temperature and refrigerate in 2- or 4-cup quantities for up to 1 week. The stock may also be frozen for up to 4 months.

Vegetable Broth

2 carrots, washed and roughly chopped

2 stalks celery, roughly chopped

1 fennel bulb, trimmed and roughly chopped

2 large yellow onions, peeled and quartered

1 bunch fresh flat-leaf parsley

4 sprigs fresh thyme

1 bay leaf

4½ quarts water

In a large stockpot, combine the carrots, celery, fennel, onions, parsley, thyme, and bay leaf. Place the pan over medium-high heat, add the water, and bring to a boil. Adjust the heat so the liquid simmers gently and cook for 1½ hours, topping up with cold water occasionally to keep the liquid at about the same level.

Strain through a fine-mesh sieve into a large, clean saucepan. Bring the stock to a boil and adjust the heat so the liquid simmers briskly, then cook until it is reduced by half, about 25 minutes. Use immediately as directed in the recipe or cool to room temperature as quickly as possible and refrigerate in 2- or 4-cup quantities for up to 1 week. The stock may also be frozen for up to 4 months.

Light Fish Broth

5 pounds fish bones
(whitefish from the sea
only; no salmon)

4 leek greens, roughly chopped
and rinsed thoroughly

2 large yellow onions,
peeled and quartered

5 stalks celery, roughly
chopped

1 bay leaf

4 quarts water

In a large stockpot, combine the fish bones, leek greens, onions, celery, and bay leaf. Add the water and bring to a boil over high heat; skim off the foam and impurities. Adjust the heat so the water simmers gently and cook for 30 minutes.

Strain through a fine-mesh sieve into a large, clean saucepan. Simmer briskly over medium-high heat until the liquid has reduced by half to about 2 quarts, 15 to 20 minutes. Use as directed in the recipe or cool to room temperature and refrigerate in 2- or 4-cup quantities for up to 1 week. The stock may also be frozen for up to 4 months.

Rich Beef Broth

This stock cooks overnight. Before you go to bed, add cold water all the way up to the rim of the stockpot, and ensure that the heat is as low as possible. Use a flame-tamer if your stove does not maintain extra-low temperatures efficiently. (This tool helps to keep the heat level at a very low and steady level, which most home stoves are unable to achieve.) Then top up with cold water again in the morning, always degreasing with a large, flat spoon.

8 pounds beef knuckles and shanks

1½ cups tomato paste

5 large carrots, washed and roughly chopped

5 large yellow onions, peeled and quartered

5 stalks celery, roughly chopped

Preheat the oven to 400°F. Place the bones in a large roasting pan and roast in the oven without turning until golden brown, about 1 hour. Spoon the tomato paste over the top of the bones and roast for 15 minutes more. Transfer the bones and the tomato paste to a 10-quart stockpot and set aside.

Wipe all the grease from the roasting pan with paper towels and add the carrots, onions, and celery. Roast for 30 minutes, then transfer all the vegetables to the stockpot.

Add enough water to come within about 2 inches of the rim and place over high heat. Bring to a boil and then adjust the heat to keep the liquid at a bare simmer (use a flame-tamer disk if your stove does not reliably stay at very low heat). Simmer for 12 hours, topping up with cold water occasionally to keep the liquid at approximately the same level. Whenever you add the cold water, degrease the stock with a large flat spoon. Strain through a fine-mesh sieve into a large, clean saucepan. Place the pan over medium-high heat and simmer briskly until reduced to about 3 quarts, degreasing occasionally as you reduce, 30 to 45 minutes. Use as directed or cool to room temperature as quickly as possible and refrigerate in 2- or 4-cup quantities for up to 1 week, or freeze for up to 6 months.

Index

Page numbers in *italics* indicate illustrations.

Photo by Nancy Ellison.

Lorraine Wallace had two great passions growing up—riding horses and cooking. She became an expert in both. Moving to Middleburg, Virginia in the 1980s, she became a competitor on the amateur show-jumping circuit and won awards on her horse, Strait Man.

At the same time, she started her own extensive garden—growing vegetables, herbs, and flowers. She developed an appreciation for organic ingredients and a deep love for cooking.

In 1997, she married Chris Wallace and moved to Washington, D.C. With Chris' four children from a previous marriage and two of her own, Lorraine had her hands full bringing the two families together. Many of the key moments that helped the family bond were around the kitchen table, where Lorraine fed her extended family. In this book, she tells the story of how soup—even if it didn't solve all their problems—made everything better.